The Diary of a Teenage Health Freak

It was his biology teacher, Mrs Smellie, who started it all off. There he was, minding his own business – feeling his pulse and wondering if his heart would hold out to the end of the lesson – when she dropped the bombshell: he was a 'hypochondriac'! Struck down by a dreaded disease, at the tender age of 14! For Pete Payne, the race was on to find out more…

Pete's 'first-hand' research extends to finding out all there is to know about subjects as diverse as masturbation, acne, diet, alcohol, drugs, depression, sex, his feelings for his girlfriend Cills, and generally surviving his crazed life with his parents and two sisters. For the next year he confides all this – and much, much more – to his diary, as he greedily devours medical facts from any source he can lay his hands on.

When Pete's diary was first unleashed on the world, the results were electrifying: teenagers grabbed it from their friends; relieved teachers and appalled parents were to be seen surreptitiously checking the latest facts.

In a generous response to enormous international pressure, Pete has now divulged the most complete and up-to-date version of his diary in all its gory detail: essential reading for all teenagers who want to know but are too embarrassed to ask, and for all adults who know some of it but are too embarrassed to answer.

D1472213

'...excellent and altogether BRILLIANT!'

'I pissed myself laughing... tells us the things my friends and I have always wanted to know, without the embarrassing idea of having to ask someone.'

'...was so good that I couldn't put it down: I read it until two in the morning and couldn't get up in time to do my paper round! ...essential for all teenagers and parents'

'...glad someone at last has the guts to write out funny or rude things you wouldn't say in the public supermarket'

The Diary of a

TEENAGE
HEALTH
FREAK

Aidan Macfarlane
and
Ann McPherson

Illustrated by John Astrop

OXFORD
UNIVERSITY PRESS

OXFORD

UNIVERSITY PRESS

Great Clarendon Street, Oxford OX2 6DP

Oxford University Press is a department of the University of Oxford.
It furthers the University's objective of excellence in research, scholarship,
and education by publishing worldwide in

Oxford New York

Auckland Bangkok Buenos Aires Cape Town Chennai
Dar es Salaam Delhi Hong Kong Istanbul Karachi Kolkata
Kuala Lumpur Madrid Melbourne Mexico City Mumbai Nairobi
São Paulo Shanghai Singapore Taipei Tokyo Toronto

with an associated company in Berlin

Oxford is a registered trade mark of Oxford University Press
in the UK and in certain other countries

First edition published in 1987
Second edition (under the title *The New Diary of a Teenage Health Freak*) 1996
This edition first published in 2002

British Library Cataloguing in Publication Data available

ISBN 0-19-910905-2

3 5 7 9 10 8 6 4

Printed in the UK
by Cox & Wyman Ltd, Reading, Berkshire

Contents

AIDAN MACFARLANE ran the Child and Adolescent Health services for the Oxfordshire Health Authority. He is now an international freelance consultant in child and adolescent health.

ANN McPHERSON is a general practitioner with extensive experience of young people and their problems, and a lecturer in the Department of Primary Health Care at the University of Oxford.

As well as *The Diary of a Teenage Health Freak* and its sequel *The Diary of the Other Health Freak*, their other books include *Mum I Feel Funny* (which won the Times Education Supplement Information Book Award), *Me and My Mates*, *The Virgin Now Boarding*, and *Fresher Pressure*. Most recently they published a book for parents about the teenage years called *Teenagers: the agony, the ecstasy, the answers*.

The authors also run an extremely successful website for teenagers – www.teenagehealthfreak.org – which receives over 150,000 hits a week and recently won the BUPA communication award.

Acknowledgements

For this, the third edition, we would like to thank our researcher, Cathy Boyd, and the thousands of teenagers who have emailed our website, www.teenagehealthfreak.org, with their concerns and views on teenage life today. Special thanks also to Oscar Leonard, and Stella, Athene and Thomas Dilke, who went through the book word by word making sure that the language was 'appropriate' for today's teenagers. Also many, many thanks to all the other teenagers who have, over the years, appreciated the books and freely given their opinions of what was both good and bad about them.

Like the previous editions, this edition was once again much aided and abetted by our own children, Beth, Gus, Magnus, Sam, Tess and Tamara, and their friends – who often continued to surprise us with their teenage revelations about their own experiences with sex, drugs, alcohol, divorce and much else besides.

Much of the original material in this book was provided by the 4th-year pupils at Lord Williams, Cheney and Peers Upper Schools in Oxfordshire. We would like to thank them and their overworked and underpaid teachers. Thanks also to Isis Middle School, Ravenspark Academy, Kate Roberts, Alice Coulter, Laura Harris, Alice Maclennan, Michael and Niall Paulin, and many other teachers and teenagers – too numerous to mention – who responded so positively when we approached them for suggestions on updating the text.

About this Diary's Writer

GENERAL INFORMATION

My name Peter H. (daren't tell you the rest) Payne.

Nickname 'Know-all Pete'.

Date of birth 17th December.

Age 14 years and 1 month – year 9 at school.

Born according to my Mum, half-way down the corridor at the hospital, on the way to the labouratory room.

Address 18 Clifton Road, Hawsley, London.

Hobbies picking my nose, watching telly, computer games, worrying about myself, teasing my younger sister and hacking into her emails, annoying people by being a know-all, collecting medical facts, reading FHM, having accidents, my body – tackle and all.

Heroes David Beckham, Nelson Mandela, myself, Sam's dad, whoever it was discovered penicillin but I can't remember who it was, Lara Croft, Harry Potter, Buffy.

What I'll be when I grow up myself, a famous scientist, very rich, and very, very attractive to girls.

Personality at the moment shy, awkward, unattractive to girls, afraid of life, shirker at washing up, tease (especially of my sister Susie), bad at sport, bit of a nerd (doing homework before watching telly), trying to be cool.

Worries catching Aids, GCSEs, growing up and having a really boring job.

PHYSICAL MAKE-UP

Sex male and becoming more so.

Height 5 feet 4 inches against my door.

Weight 58 kilos but ate a big dinner.

Hair colour brown.

Eye colour brown to match.

Distinguishing marks the whole of me but especially the brown birthmark on my bum which I want to show to my girlfriend Cills.

MY MUM

Name Jane Elspeth Margaret.

Date of birth June – sometime but can't remember exact date and Mum says she doesn't have birthdays anyhow.

Age 35 for the last 6 years.

Job part-time in local doctor's surgery, cook, cleaner, clothes washer, general neighbourhood 'do-gooder', Mum to us all, including Dad (or most of all Dad).

Weight chubby (but I never said it).

Hair colour brown.

Eye colour green with flecks.

Distinguishing marks her laugh, like a sick hyena.

Personality noses into my private life all the time, makes me be nice to stupid relations, doesn't take any notice when I have sleeping problems etc. and just says 'you'll get over it', is always saying 'have you done your homework?', but is cuddly, a good listener, and doesn't bother me about my room the way Sam's mum does.

MY DAD

Name Anthony Tobias.

Date of birth don't know.

Age nobody knows.

Job kills tiny beasties in people's houses. It's called 'pest control', which is what I do to my sister Susie.

Weight expanding in the middle.

Hair disappearing on top.

Eye colour can't remember.

Distinguishing marks awful moustache.

Personality funny, good at mending broken things, won't stop smoking but does it secretly, always talking politics, knows about a lot of things.

MY OLDER SISTER

Name Sally (and Beatrix – TOP SECRET).

Date of birth keep forgetting.

Age 18.

Weight a state secret.

Hair colour changes all the time.

Eye colour blue.

Distinguishing marks two bouncy ones in front.

Personality worse know-all than me, bossy, and will do almost anything for money, which she's saving up to buy a motorbike with.

Favourite music Chemical Brothers, Manic Street Preachers, Robbie Williams – makes me want to puke.

MY YOUNGER SISTER

Name Susie Jane (lucky her – they'd run out of awful names).

Date of birth tells us about 6 times a day – 16th January.

Age 12 years and 11 months.

Hair colour mousy.

Eye colour mousy too – like the rest of her.

Distinguishing marks none.

Personality worries about what her friends will think of her family, emails everyone and everything that moves, enjoys shopping, giggles, doesn't obey my orders, and overreacts on purpose when I tell her off, especially if Mum's around.

MY BROTHER

Sad – Mum and Dad never gave me one.

MY BEST FRIENDS

Name Sam Sproggs.

Sex says he's male.

Age claims he's 14. Most of the time behaves like he's 4 or 40.

Personality crazy about bicycles, attractive to girls (Susie quite fancies him) but ignores them, tries to be original but isn't, gets more pocket money than me.

Name Eddie Marley

Sex male

Age 14

Personality outstanding – great skateboarder and roller-blader, and even greater at footie. Occasional weirdo – seems to fancy my sister Susie.

ROMANTIC ATTACHMENTS

Name Cilla Jeffs.

Sex yes, if she'll let me.

Age 14.

Where she lives not saying.

Why I like her just do.

PETS

Type cat (Sally's) which would starve to death if Mum didn't feed her.

Name Bovril.

Age 14 demented months and losing all her hair.

MY HOUSE

Semi-detached with more bays than the south coast. Metal round the windows like every other house for miles around. Three bedrooms and a shoe-box for Susie. Pink tiles in the bathroom. Fitted carpets everywhere. Hairs on Mum's settee where Bov the cat's been. Kitchen fixtures care of Dad, so not finished yet.

MY ROOM

'IN and OUT' message board on the outside of the door, and paper skeleton on the inside. Bed with all my old clothes down the back. Pooh Bear one million times over on my bedcover. Dad's yellow paint over bumpy wallpaper, picture of aeroplane by me, covered with Lara Croft and Buffy pictures. Books and comics everywhere.

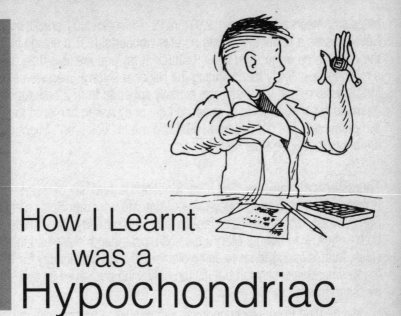

How I Learnt I was a Hypochondriac

Tuesday 8th January Trouble, trouble, trouble. Was messaging my friend Sam 'R U OK 4 footie Sat?' on my new mobile (Christmas prezzie from Mum and Dad – better me with fried brain than them violent with my nagging, they reckoned) when nearly got mugged by a couple of drunks. Ran for it as I didn't want 24,000 stolen mobiles to be 24,001. Won't show off with it in public anymore – I reckon.

Wednesday 9th January Biology teacher set me off today. Going on and on about how wonderful and efficient our heart is – 80 beats per minute, 3 billion pumps during a whole lifetime. Estimated mine's already done 80 times 60 times 24 times 365 times 14 = 588,672,000 beats. (My calculator ran out of space – need a better one.) Worried about all this work my heart's already done; felt sure it would never last out. Asked Mrs Smellie whether I was likely to have a heart attack in the afternoon's cross-country run cos my Grandad died of a heart attack running for a bus last year. Know he was 80 but dead worried it might run in the family. Smellie said not to be stupid. Exercise is good for the heart and helps stop heart attacks when we're older – just like NOT smoking does. Never misses a chance of telling us how wonderful NOT smoking is. Said the odds of me dying from a heart attack at my age are less than one in a million – less likely than winning the National Lottery. Even worse was Mrs Smellie remarking that I was actually suffering from a bad attack of 'teenage hypochondriasis' – suppose I die of it? Asked her what the symptoms are, but got nowhere. Just told me to 'look it up'. Might get around to it, if I don't die first.

Thursday 10th January Still alive. Managed a third day of diary! Nothing much happened today except I got into my sister Susie's email. She's invited Kate as well as Mary for her 13th birthday party. I hate them both – they're so boring. Mary's the sixth 'best friend' she's had in a week. Mum's taking them to some dismal girly film on Monday for the fourth time. Really babyish but it's the only thing on. Saved by text message from Sam 'On 4 Sat'.

Haven't died from hypochondriasis disease yet – perhaps it's not as serious as I thought. Sam's dad will know – he's an expert.

Saturday 12th January Hypochondriasis thing is beginning to worry me. Sneaked into the school library at lunchtime yesterday and got the dictionary down to find out about the dreaded disease...it might be catching and I'll never be able to get close to Cills again. Looked up 'EROGENOUS' instead. 'Areas of the body causing sexual excitement, such as nipples, ear lobes, and the inside of the thighs.' Made me think of Cills, so had to ditch book and make rapid exit.

Helped Dad mend the car today. Wish we had an Audi TT like Sam's dad instead of our decaying rust bucket. Could be worse, though – could have a boring Volvo Estate like Randy Joe's dad. Ours sounds as though it's dying of lung cancer – a bit like Dad coughing in the mornings after a 40-a-day fag binge. We had to get it started to go for lunch with Aunty Pam tomorrow. Wish Dad would put it out of its misery and get a proper one instead.

Met Sam later and cycled over to watch his team play football. You'd have thought I was Scott, off to the Antarctic, the way Mum insisted I wrap up – 'so you won't catch cold'. Embarrassing and hardly streamlined, even on my old bike. Sam's got a new Scott mountain bike and was wearing Catscan glasses. What a tosser and he wouldn't even let me try de wunda bike – says I'll bust it, and as his dad paid over a grand for it, not too surprised, though all his fancy Lance Armstrong type gear is a bit much. Prefer my board and Rip Curl gear myself.

Sam's team won but the goalkeeper broke a leg, and will be out for the rest of the season. Heard the crack as it went. Left before the visiting thugs (don't know why they call them fans) were let loose from their cages. Not that I'm a coward, just hate violence, particularly if it's me getting hurt. Cycled home at top speed to help my heart pump the way it should (estimate I am near the 600 million mark now). Slowed down again in case it made the hypochondriasis worse.

Sam came to tea and dribbled jam all over the sofa of Mum's new three-piece suite. Had to lick it off, cat hairs and all. Sam loves coming to tea with us. At his house he's never allowed to have white bread, chips, bacon and egg, tomato ketchup, chocolate biscuits, or coke. Maybe Mum's not so bad after all; or maybe I have this hypochondriasis thing cos I eat so bad.

Susie's a pain when Sam's around – always trying to talk to him and show off, even trying to join in conversations about footie and bikes, as if SHE knows anything about them. She used to hate my friends, but now she's suddenly all over them – is this what the books call 'PUBERTY'? Couldn't she just stick to girls? Don't fancy a lesbian for a sister, but what's that make Sam and me?

Argument about telly with Mum. Lost as usual. The same old things – it strains your eyes, makes them red, makes you bad-tempered, gives you a headache, makes you violent, turns you into a sex maniac (told her I already was one, which didn't help much), I don't get enough sleep, I always watch rubbish – and anyway, I'd already watched the football on Sky Sports. She said Dad should never have got cable. She'd prefer to be like Sam's parents, who refuse to have lean, mean Rupert Murdoch beamed into their front room.

Still worrying about THE DISEASE.

Sunday 13th January Forced up by Mum at 12 o'clock. Still furious with her about the telly. Such a hypocrite – she watches rubbish *Eastenders*. Mum and Dad just don't understand. First they say I need a lot of sleep and then they complain when I stay in bed late. Their problem is that they can't make up their minds.

Car-sick on journey to Aunty Pam's. Susie read all the way. How can SHE do it without feeling sick? It's not fair. Mum wouldn't let me sit in the front and no one wanted the window open cos of the cold – till I said I was about to throw up.

Aunty Pam's place smells awful – dog shit, cat pee, beer on Uncle Bob's breath, Aunty Pam kissing me with all that sickly powder and perfume! There should be a law against grown-ups kissing children over 12, so I told Aunt Pam that you can get Aids from kissing (though I know this isn't true). Always knew I couldn't stand Uncle Bob; now I know why. First thing he said was, 'I notice you've got a bit of a moustache, young man'. As if you could call the growth on my upper lip a moustache, and anyhow I've devoted a lot of effort to NOT noticing it. Susie and Mum laughed and I made things worse by blushing. Bad enough having this hypochondriasis, without my other blemishes being pointed out.

Asked Susie whether any of her friends had this hypochondriasis disease. She said, yes, lots – and what I actually was, was a hypochondriac. Bloody know-all, worse than me, but didn't dare admit I didn't know what it meant.

Monday 14th January Went round to Sam's. His dad's a medical expert doing research with animals into stuff like genes. Wonder if he read all about medical things when he was my age? Hoped he'd reveal all about 'hypochondriasis' – he seems to know about everything, but he was away at a conference. Sam says that's where he goes whenever he needs a rest.

Susie had her friends for a birthday supper after their film while I was out. Kate's invited Susie for next holidays. Good.

Tuesday 15th January GREAT DAY. Got to school early. Amazed everybody including myself. Arrived just as Whitton, the caretaker, was opening up. Very surprised to see ME at that time – normally catches me sneaking in the back way after the bell's gone. Usually find myself tripping over a crowd of 6th-formers smoking. Told Whitton I'd some work to do in the library. Took down the dictionary with clammy palms – and here we were. 'HYDROPHOBIA – an aversion to water, especially as a symptom of rabies.' Help, this was something else I had got – I hate baths. 'HYPNOSIS – state like sleep in which subject acts only on external suggestion.' Began to wonder whether I had everything in the dictionary. 'HYPOCHONDRIASIS – abnormal anxiety about one's health.' So that's all it is. I'm a person who has an abnormal anxiety about his health and not a deadly disease.

Relief – though I have to admit that there IS a bit of this in me, cos thinking back, in a way I was disappointed there was nothing serious wrong. Had begun to see myself lying in hospital with piles of choccies and grapes, my family and friends by my bed: Mum all in anguish for not letting me watch more telly, Dad promising to give up his fags, and Sam really sorry he hadn't let me ride his new bike. Can see how a hypochondriac's life could be a happy one.

Crashing the
Pain Barrier
on a Bike

Tuesday 22nd January Exhausted by NOT having TEENAGE HYPOCHONDRIAC DISEASE, so have given up on my diary writing resolution. But am still hacking into to Sister Susie's emails…though all she does is tell her friends that I fancy Lara Croft.

Wednesday 30th January Had a major accident and am stuck indoors, so am starting to write diary again.

Last Saturday started off OK. Sam called, and we went off on our bikes to visit a friend of ours called Jo, as Sam wanted to show her how to text-message him luvvie stuff. They disappeared upstairs, leaving me feeling a right jerk. Then Nick, another friend of ours, arrived and took my bike, so for a laugh I rode Sam's new Scott mountain bike round the close. Being fairly short in the leg department, I couldn't really handle it. Going downhill, I suddenly couldn't find the brakes – result: sheer panic, which didn't help. At the bottom was a row of houses and a sharp left turn. Still searching for the brakes, I hit the curb at about 100 mph and flew over the handlebars (a bit like big ears Charlie boy off his polo pony). Heard something go CRACK – a sound I'd heard not too long ago on a footie pitch – and that was that.

Next thing I remember was being in an ambulance. The driver and his mate were laughing and telling jokes. Couldn't understand what had happened. My new Moschino jeans were ripped at the bum, my left arm was blown up in a plastic bag so I couldn't move it, and my head hurt like hell. Things were coming and going, and I felt sick and faint like after the last lunch Aunty Pam cooked for me. But there were no sirens blaring…big disappointment. The paramedics said they only used them in real emergencies – like when they were starving for their tea.

Finally we stopped, and when they opened the back doors, there was Mum, crying, and Dad, white-faced. Dad started swearing and telling me what a bloody stupid thing it was to do, and had I done it on purpose to worry them, and why didn't I think about these things before I did them? Honest, grown-ups! I was nearly dying, and here he was shouting like an axe-murdering maniac. Mum told him to shut up. Wanted to get out of the ambulance all by my selfdom to show I was all OK, but the paramedics wrapped me up in a red blanket like I was 80 or something, and carried me out in a sort of chair. They said I'd broken my arm and the blown-up plastic bag was to keep the bits together and stop it hurting. Mum clutched my good hand and Dad dragged along behind, muttering about Sam being furious over the scratches on his bike.

They wheeled me into a little white room and put me on a hard bed so that my Nokia with its new blue front bit stuck into the gash on my bum and I screamed. Just as well I hadn't landed on the other back pocket or my mobile would've been a goner too. Mum had to go out and ask if I could have something for the pain – and came back saying that the nurse was sorry but they were busy. Mum muttered about the NHS always being wait, wait, wait nowadays, what with Tony B being too busy with other things like his holidays.

At last a nurse came and shoved a thermometer in my mouth (glad it wasn't my bum) and held my wrist. Wasn't as pretty as the nurses on telly, though she was certainly as nice. Helped me take my torn jeans off, which was dead embarrassing as I hadn't changed my boxers for a couple of days and they were a bit whiffy. My poor, poor legs were all white and covered in grazes. My heart nearly stopped when I thought she was going to ask me to take off my boxers as well.

Then a man came in and asked me questions about the accident, and some silly things like what day was it and who was the prime minister – how dumb can you get? He looked into my eyes with a light, stuck pins into my legs (as if they didn't hurt enough already) to see if I could feel anything – so I yelled. Then he took off my boxers and examined EVERY last bit of me. Cills will be glad to know – no damage THERE. Finally felt brave enough to ask what he was doing. He said it was to make sure I hadn't done any damage to my brain – like being concussed. Susie said 'No chance, he hasn't got one'. Decided to cull all sisters.

Nobody seemed to have actually DONE anything to make me better till another lady came in and started examining me ALL OVER again. 'Oi! – get off me boxers', I said, but she turned out to be the proper doctor and the other guy was just some medical student. She explained that she was going to arrange for my head to be X-rayed to make sure none of my head bones were broken, and to X-ray my arm cos she was sure that that was broken. Suddenly I wanted to be home in my own bed.

The lady doctor showed me the X-rays and said I was lucky not to have dented my skull and damaged my brain. Said she couldn't understand why people didn't wear crash helmets when cycling, because around 160 cyclists are killed and 23,000 injured in England and Wales each year. Told me that if I was thinking of getting a motorcycle in the future, I'd HAVE to wear one – as if I didn't know that already. But even so, 500 motorcyclists were killed on the roads last year, and 24,500 injured. She was a bit fed up as she spent most of every day putting bits of people together after they had had accidents, and in England every year:

1 in every 24 motorcycle riders
1 in every 107 car drivers

are killed or involved in an accident. Not even safe to walk around, as 900 pedestrians are killed and 43,000 injured each year. All this doesn't even include other types of accidents like drowning, which kills over 40 children a year, or the 2.8 million-plus people treated in hospital for home accidents each year. HELP! HELP – maybe I should stay in hospital – must be safe there.

Asked the doc if SHE wore a crash helmet when she cycled. She went silent and didn't answer. Mum gave me one of her special looks and said I shouldn't be cheeky. Dad went back to work and Mum stayed while they put sloppy wet white bandages on my arm which made it warm. Bit by bit the bandages grew hard and smooth, and I was left with a hard shiny white plaster for my friends to write on. Doc said it was to stop the ends of my broken bones moving so that they can heal properly. Said they might replace it with a fibreglass splint after a week or so.

Just as I thought everyone was finished, there was one more thing – an anti-tetanus injection. The dirt in the cuts on my knee might have contained tetanus bacteria. This could give me lockjaw, which is spasm of the muscles of your body, not just your jaw, and can easily kill you. Mum said I had last had the injection when I was 5 but that it only protects you against tetanus for about 10 years and then you need it again. I said I'd had a jab at school last term, but apparently that was against measles or something. Asked the doctor whether the needle was clean as I didn't want to catch Aids whilst I was in there, but the doc said they use a new one every time.

Cos I'd been knocked out, they said I might have to stay in hospital for the night. Dead frightened about this, but then thought it might be fun, specially if all my friends came to see me with presents. However, was allowed home with Mum because everything seemed OK, but they told her she should bring me back if I began to throw up, had a bad headache, saw double, or became drowsy because of the knock on my head. They also said to come back if the fingers of my broken arm got numb, swelled up, or became white or blue. Sounded dead nasty but didn't happen.

Last four days have been boring, boring – Playstation absolutely no fun with only one hand – which is why I am writing all this instead.

Nobody's been to see me except Sam – to complain about his bike. Why hasn't Cills come to hold my good hand and tell me how brave I am? – that's what I want to know. All Sam did was to go on about how some new girl called Beth in our class was soft on him – which didn't improve my sex life one bit. Dad said that I've suffered enough and that he'd pay for the repairs to Sam's bike. He can be great sometimes – though it turned out Sam's bike was all insured, so he didn't have to cough up. Susie and Sal have been real sympathetic too, so I reckon having sisters isn't all bad.

Friday 1st February Up early to catch the bus – first day back at school. Was the centre of attention for all of 5 secs while everyone (except Cills) defaced my plaster with graffiti, which now I feel embarrassed to be carrying around in public. Pity I haven't got one of those new lightweight fibreglass ones yet.

Had to sit out and work during the sports periods. Don't usually like sport but now I can't do it, I feel left out. Mr Jones, the sports teacher, is orgasmic about exercise and says we could be almost mega-fit if we did at least 20 minutes exercise three times a week, enough to make us sweat. Seeing that I had nothing better to do, he said I'd better be the form representative for the school magazine and get some articles for the next edition.

Finally got the chance to tell my mates about my accident (went over the top a bit about my bravery and my attractiveness to the nurses). But I could hardly get a word in cos everyone else thought they'd had a worse accident than me and they were going to tell me about it whatever happened. So fed up that I told them to write about their troubles for the school magazine.

Thursday 7th February Have had a whole week without writing. Too exhausted by my one-handed efforts at home and in school. Lucky I'm not into my GCSEs yet, specially as all the teachers have stopped making allowances for the fact that I'm a cripple. Stories for magazine about people's accidents coming in well. The things my form mates seem to get up to...

• •

'Was playing 40-40 up the shop with my sister and a friend about 4 years ago. I ran out across the road to get 'in' and a big red bus hit me just as it was going to stop. My sister went to get my mum. She came running out and I was just running round and round. The doctor came and he got me and my mum to the hospital. I slept in the hospital for the night. I just had a bit of concussion. I went home next day.'   *Giti*

• •

'I broke my nose right across the bridge. I was standing with my brother and he was shaking the rain off his hair and I walked into him and broke my nose. It gave me headaches, and a purple and very embarrassing nose. I went to the hospital and first they said I would have to wait till the swelling went down. Then they sent me to the Ear, Nose and Throat clinic. No one was really sympathetic about it.'   *Tim*

• •

'About 3 years ago I was hoovering in the hallway. A piece of paper would not go up the hoover, so I pushed it in with a knife, and my fingers got sucked in and all cut up. Also, when I was about 10, I was sitting on the sink in the bathroom and it fell off the wall and I hit my eye and it was all bleeding.'   *Jo*

• •

'I've had at least three accidents but none of them serious. The first was when I got kicked by my pony at a show, but I wasn't hurt badly, only bruised and slightly sore. Then I was bitten by another pony while I was doing up his girth. This hurt more than when I was kicked, because it cut the skin and I was bleeding. Another accident was when I fell off and got dragged along the road. I was riding a small pony, taking her back to the field, when

11

two girls came running down the road and startled her and she darted under a low branch and knocked me off. I clung on to the reins and she dragged me along for quite a way. I hurt all of one side and I still have the scars.'　　　**Sharon**

'Me and another girl went for a walk by this railway line. There were three boys chucking stones and one big stone landed on my head. They rushed me to hospital. I lost 3 pints of blood and had to have 16 stitches – 6 inside and 10 outside. They had to give me 5 injections in my head to make the skin numb when they stitched me up. I had to stay in hospital overnight, and when my parents came and told me the news I started crying, so the doctors let me go home. My sister was there when the stone was in my head and my cousin, who pulled the stone out, said she could see my skull bone. The doctors and my parents thought I was going to die because if the cut had split any more I would have been gone. Now every time I see people throwing stones I run indoors and I think that that fear will always stay with me. If anyone hits me round my head or touches it, I go mad and throw out at them.'　　　**Liz**

'My last injury was just over a month ago when I went ice-skating for the first time. I can roller-blade, but I had been told by my friends that it was harder because you slip over everywhere. I went skating with some of my friends, but when I got on to the ice I was very frightened because when I tried to move I slipped over. Then everything was going great until a boy behind me pushed me over and I went crashing into the side of the rink. As I did this, I put my hand on the floor. Some boy who was standing next to me skated over my fingers. I started crying because I was in a great deal of pain. My friends saw me and helped me off the rink. My fingers were pouring with blood and all the skin was ripped back and my nail was cracked and bruised. After the accident I decided never to go skating again – but I did.'   **Judy**

....

'My last injury was when I electrocuted my right hand. It happened when I turned on this lamp. I had been using nail varnish to make the bulb red. The effect of the burn on me was that I couldn't write for a month. I had to go to hospital as it was an electric burn, which apparently is much worse. I had to have plastic surgery and the skin was taken from the outer part of my other hand. I was in hospital for 3 days.'   **Daniel**

....

'When I was 10, I put my hand through a window. A chunk of skin came out and I was rushed to hospital. I was told I had to have a skin graft. I didn't know what that was then, and now I wish I hadn't had it because I'm still scarred and I think that I will be scarred for life. It is very embarrassing because the skin was taken from the smooth surface of my arm, and you can still see it.'   **Sonja**

....

'I was on a bike coming down a hill. I was with a friend who was in front of me. A car was in front of my friend. He went right into the door as it opened and flew over the door and hit his head as he landed. I went up the back of him and went over the handlebars, swearing like anything at the driver. I came down with my leg underneath my bike, and my other leg twisted round the handlebars and the brake cable. The bloke got out of his car and said my friend was all right, and I told him what I thought of him. My friend got up and was slightly concussed but not much. I got hold of his bike and carried it home and then went off to the police station with my dad and my friend's dad. It has confirmed my feelings about people who do not look properly before opening their car doors.'   **Tony**

....

13

'I had an accident on my bike and twisted my bollocks and had to have 60 stitches in my bollock bag...'

Anon (I think it's Randy Joe)

••

I made sure this last one didn't get into the magazine cos I reckoned Randy Joe was just trying to boast about his bollock bag and nothing else.

Friday 8th February Nose bleed after sitting on the bog picking it. Blood everywhere. Thought I was dying again.

Feeling Real **Fed Up**

Wednesday 13th February Big bust-up between Mum and Dad last night. Something to do with Gran and camping in the summer, and how she always insists on bringing her spare false teeth with her in a plastic bag, and Dad not wanting to have the police having to search for them again. Seemed OK this morning though, but they wouldn't tell us about it. When I asked, was told by Dad not to pick up fag ends. That's rich coming from someone who pretends to have given up smoking! Didn't choose to answer back though. Am cycling to school again after 2 weeks on the bus cos of my bust arm. Glad to get rid of my arm plaster but still scared by what the doc said at the hospital about my fingers going numb or blue, as my hand still hurts. Everyone at school crowded round and Cills, who I really like, wanted to touch my arm. 'Cos', she said, 'it looks all white and pathetic', and then she spoilt it by adding '...like the rest of you'. Kill, kill.

Usual chaos in French. Miss Dunlop is hopeless at keeping order. Sam and I sat at the back discussing our summer plans for cycling and camping. Told him about Gran. Were caught chatting – my first detention tomorrow, so maybe my friends will reckon I'm not such a boff after all.

Friday 15th February Sent a massive 23 Valentine emails and 12 text messages yesterday. Absolutely zilch back…except one text message I was sure was from Mum which said 'Luv u always XXX your little snugglebuggles XXX'. But then again Mum doesn't have a mobile and has never sent a text message in her life. Turned out it was from Sam, which wasn't all bad cos I sent him one as well just for fun…or was it? Maybe I'm gay or something?

Tuesday 19th February Mum and Dad at one another again this evening. Sally made it worse by saying she was going to be out late. Mum said she should ask, not tell, and what about that last bit of AS-level coursework? Sally flounced out saying that all her friends were allowed to stay out late, even on weekdays. Her parting shot was that she was not only old enough to get married, but also old enough to have a baby. Shook Mum rigid. I beat hasty retreat to write this in my diary. Heard Sal coming in early, slamming the front door meaningfully, so maybe she hasn't been baby-making.

Seems Mum's got more control over Sally than over Bov the cat though, who's been out all night waking the neighborhood with her sex life. At least she's got one — which is more than me!

Wednesday 20th February Dead worried that I'd got meningitis as I woke with a headache but have had the jab at school. In such a state nearly mistook Mum's sleeping tablets for paracetamol, and forgot my maths book. Was late meeting Sam, who was dead upset in spite of the fact I had texted him 'B late mate'. He disappeared with other friends at break, and I had no one to talk to. Finally had to stay on for my detention. Not only bored with all my work at school but couldn't even be bothered with my Playstation when I got home. But at least the headache's gone.

Thursday 21st February Sal spent hours in the bathroom tarting herself up for Mike, her latest boyfriend, while everyone else hung around waiting. Susie's been moaning about having no friends. Getting into her email, I found that her ex-best friend Kate has found a new best friend — don't blame her. Susie yelled at me for not passing the sugar at tea-time. She's too fat to have it anyway. Turns out Beth's asked Sam to the cinema on Friday, and what's more he's going. Thought I was going with him but he texted me '2moro off – don't want 3sum Thx TTFN'. He seems to like Beth more than me and, much as I want to, I'm too shy to ask Cills. Maybe I really am gay cos I'd rather go with Sam.

Friday 22nd February Pouring rain – got soaked going to school. Both Mum and my maths teacher asked me if I had got out of bed the wrong side. Felt exhausted and had a headache all day, and was still fed up with the thought of not going to the film with Sam.

Then came the BIG bust-up – like Israel and Palestine, but serious. I'd spilt some tea by mistake. Susie said it was on purpose cos it was her

turn to clear and wash up, and that I had to wipe it up. Didn't see why I should as it was HER turn. She made a face and stomped to the kitchen with a pile of dishes. So I spilt her tea, and when she came back told her now she had something to clear up. She tried to hit me. I caught and twisted her arm. She fell and hit the table and a glass of milk fell and smashed on the floor. Mum appeared looking black as thunder. Told her it was all Susie's fault and Susie, lying as usual, said it was all mine. Mum threw a washing-up cloth at Susie and a brush at me, telling us to get on with clearing it up. Then she walked out in a real strop.

Didn't stop Susie though, who slopped milk over my new trainers, whispering 'I hate you', so I told her she was a real pain and no wonder Kate didn't like her any more. Knew for certain that this would provoke violence. She hit me on the arm with her milk-sodden tea towel, so I screamed and collapsed (unhurt) on the floor clutching my arm and shouting she'd broken it again, but actually cut myself accidentally on the broken glass on the floor.

At that instant both Mum and Dad appeared – Mum at one door speechless with rage, and Dad at the other, fresh from beastie bashing, equally speechless. Mum recovered first, yelling 'BOTH TO BED – NOW.' Dad blurted out, 'Do what your mother says or I'll get in the United Nations peacekeeping force'. I cried 'But I'm bleeding', and Susie said, 'But it was all his fault, why do you always pick on ME?' 'BED', Mum screamed. Deliberately dripped blood all up the stairs, stamped up to my room, slamming the door. Lay listening to Susie sobbing. Maybe 'feeling fed up' is infectious.

What seemed hours later, Sal came up to fetch us for dinner. In Susie's room the sobbing immediately began again, followed by a shout of 'No – leave me alone, everybody hates me.' Texted her a message 'AFAIC that's not true – WAN2TLK?' Heard her stop sniffling – and got text back 'CU now downstairs'.

But supper was dead silent affair as Mum and Dad were still fuming and I hadn't energy or nerve to reject Mum's liver and green beans – even though they make me want to puke. Dad made real feeble jokes which disappeared into the generally shitty atmosphere without a ripple. Came straight up after supper to write this. Sometimes writing about things seems to make them better.

10 p.m. Thought I had finished for the day – but couldn't sleep for Mum and Dad shouting at one another and the throbbing of my cut. The argument seemed to start again with something about Gran coming on holiday, but the battlefield soon broadened out and made less sense than even Susie and me.

From all the shouting it seemed Dad never gave Mum any support looking after us, never did any cooking, washing-up or cleaning, always forgot her birthday and for that matter Valentine's Day, never put the bog seat down after peeing, never fed the cat, never washed the bath after himself, spent the whole of some nights with a headache, never wiped his feet, always left oily bits of the car all over the sitting-room sofa, and was always indulging our materialistic needs and never considering hers.

Dad, in Mum's pauses, claimed that she always left the car with no petrol in, was illogical, never appreciated the fact that he came shopping with her, always got the pages of the newspaper muddled up, never put the top back on the toothpaste and, worst of all, us children were becoming just like her…and so it went on.

Suddenly felt totally miserable and real, real worried. Were Mum and Dad going to get divorced? It would be all my fault. Had to admit, I may have started it all, when I was feeling fed up. If Mum and Dad separated, life wouldn't be worth living. We'd be passed backwards and forwards like Tom Cruise and Nicole Kidman's kids.

Wasn't tired anymore. Had to talk to somebody, anybody, about it all. Crept along to Susie's room but she wasn't there, so tried Sally's and there were Sally and Susie curled up in bed together chatting. I collapsed on the floor, close to tears, aware of the silence that had descended downstairs.

Sal then started doing her Mum act. 'Don't worry, it's not yours or Susie's fault. Grown-ups often have rows. I'm amazed you haven't heard Mum and Dad before. You two are not the only ones to quarrel, you know. An occasional row is a normal part of life, and Mum and Dad yelling doesn't mean they don't love each other. You have to know someone really well to be able to love them AND know how to hurt them too! Mike and I have terrible rows all the time, about the silliest things. But I think it's better than bottling things up, like Uncle Bob and Aunty Pam have been doing for the last 25 years. There's nothing like a good row for clearing the air. You wait and see tomorrow.'

Tried telling Sally how awful I felt, and she really seemed to know what I meant. She even put a sticky plaster on my cut.

Saturday 23rd February Woke this morning knowing it was going to be a better day – and it has been. First Dad made breakfast! And to my amazement Mum was all soppy and appreciative. Dad even kissed Mum in front of us – ugh! Mum said I looked tired and I tried to joke that I hadn't been able to sleep last night for all the noise. 'Oh,' Mum said, all innocent, 'I hope you weren't listening to our "discussion" last night'. Had to laugh, so I added that next time Susie and I had a 'discussion', please would they not interfere. Dad said not to be cheeky.

Sam came round later to complain that Beth had brought two friends with her to the cinema and that the girls had all sat together and expected him to buy them popcorn. He's gone off girls and stayed for supper.

Monday 25th February Nothing much happened on Sunday, but at school today a group of my friends were discussing parents. Eddie's parents are divorced. They had terrible rows all the time, threw things at one another, and then when his dad finally left to go back to Jamaica, no one told him the truth – his mum just said that he'd gone off for a holiday by himself. This scared the hell out of me, but sounded much worse than Mum and Dad. Eddie said that even if he wished his mum and dad were still together, it was much more peaceful now.

When I got home, Sally had left one of her magazines on my bed. It had some 'meaningful' article by a child shrink about teenagers feeling depressed.

Moods and Depression in Teenagers

Sometimes it is difficult to tell the difference between being fed up and being depressed. One tends to merge with the other. Some people see being depressed as being very, very fed up. However, we all feel fed up sometimes, and perhaps even occasionally a bit depressed. Luckily few of us suffer from severe depression. Many of the things which make us moody can seem much worse, and indeed almost insurmountable, if we are already depressed.

Listed below are some of the things which may cause you to feel this way:

* feeling very lonely or unsure of yourself
* a friend committing suicide
* your parents separating or getting divorced
* your parents having rows or arguments all the time
* feeling unable to manage your life
* one of your parents getting very depressed
* being seriously ill yourself or your parents getting ill
* having rows with your close friends
* problems and worries with your work
* your parents always expecting you to be wonderful

If several of these problems occur together, you may feel it is impossible to cope and even wonder whether it is worth while going on living. If this happens, help and treatment are available. It's much better to try to talk to

---

somebody about it rather than keep it all to yourself. The best person is somebody YOU find it easy to talk to. It may be your best friend, your mother or father, sister or brother, teacher, doctor, priest or vicar, aunt or a sympathetic friend.

It is sometimes difficult to recognize exactly when being fed up becomes being depressed, but this list might help:

* feelings of complete hopelessness and helplessness
* feeling that everything in the future is going to be bad
* feeling that the smallest task is impossible
* being very self-critical over a long time, so that you think nothing you do is ever any good
* feelings of continued tiredness over days or weeks
* being unable to sleep for many nights on end, and waking up early in the morning when this is not normal for you
* frequent headaches and/or tummy pains for which there is no obvious cause
* loss of appetite with loss of weight, or compulsive eating
* feelings of being cut off from everyone around you, including family and friends
* work suddenly seeming much more difficult to do
* staying away from school or running away from home

None of these things by themselves, or just lasting for a few hours, or a day, mean you are seriously depressed. However, it is when one or more of them occur over several weeks that this may be depression and you should then get help. It is not nice being depressed. It is like an illness and needs to be treated.

If you think one of your friends is depressed, try to get them to talk to you about how they feel. If they are feeling really bad, you ought to tell someone else about it – maybe your parents. Sometimes your friends may find it easier to talk to your parents than their own. Otherwise discuss it with a teacher or someone else you trust.

School **Gets** Busted, Pupil on **Drugs**

Monday 4th March Decided I'm not depressed, but can now recognize about five teachers at school who are. Can't blame them given what they get paid to try and educate us.

Tuesday 5th March Found a book about 'sex and puberty' in my room – wonders never cease, but how did it get there? Mum and Dad are the prime suspects.

Wednesday 6th March Real excitement. Reporters, police everywhere asking us questions. A geek called Smith in the upper 6th, who usually spends all his time bullying 50-kilo weaklings like me, has been pushing hash to year 9's. Mr Rogers found some poor kid throwing up behind the bicycle shed. Heavy interrogation by Mum when I got back. She'd heard it on the local radio news. Had he pushed it on me? Had I ever tried it? Had any of my friends? By the time she'd finished I was convinced my whole class was sniffing coke. Anyhow I know Mum takes a sleeping tablet now and again. Told her she'd better watch it or she'd become an addict herself. Got 'the look'.

Susie's ill with diarrhoea. Hope I don't catch it.

Thursday 7th March Mobiled up, and out at 7 among the joggers and the dog shit to get the local newspaper. Fame at last. Texted Sam 'Got 2 read paper 2 day'. There it all was:

Seventeen-year-old Pupil Pushing Drugs at Local Comp

A 6th-former at Wendles Secondary School was arrested yesterday for allegedly selling cannabis to junior pupils. He blamed other pupils for getting him hooked. 'First time I had it was at a friend's house. It had been all planned beforehand to get me stoned, which I was really angry about. It was not my fault. At first it was just like smoking a cigarette but getting a pleasant effect as well. I kept laughing. It was like being drunk without the sick feeling. I only smoked when I was offered the stuff at big parties. Then I met somebody who said they could get the stuff really easily. My friends started coming to get it from me. This dealer person started getting heavy and threatening me with his Yardie gang. He wanted me to start using other things, but I refused. I know what hard drugs do to people. No way would I inject or anything like that. I think that's disgusting.'

Police Inspector James said, 'That's the way some of these kids get hooked. The "hard" drug pushers start them on something like cannabis and then say, "Why don't you just sniff a bit of this?" or "Just put a bit of this in your drink". Before they know it, they're hooked on heroin, cocaine or amphetamines, though crack is probably the worst – one or two goes and they are hooked for good.'

Mr Macintosh, the headmaster of Wendles School, said he was naturally horrified, and wanted to reassure parents that nothing like this had occurred in the school before. One year 9 pupil said he thought it was disgusting. He said that if alcohol and tobacco had been discovered now, they'd also have been made illegal, and it was high time they banned smoking in the teachers' common room. Smoking and alcohol were just another kind of drug.

It was me! That's what I had said to the bloke – and they had put it in the paper! Eat your heart out, Sam. He's always trying to get one up on me. Got a text message back from him. 'Dad supports England decriminalizing cannabis like in Holland and Portugal and other places. YF Sam.'

Friday 8th March Rumours everywhere. Ecstasy being sold over the counter in the school shop. An amphetamine factory in the chemistry labs (half the school was in there today trying to find out if it was true). Mr Macintosh, the head, gave a talk at assembly. Dead silence as he started. 'It has come to my notice (hardly surprising – as it has been in the paper and on the radio!) that certain elements (did he mean us?) are bringing the school into disrepute by their activities. The staff have instructions to look out for any evidence of any kind of this evil practice of drug taking. I've already suspended one boy. Other suspensions will follow. Do not get the idea that we are soft on drugs.'

All in all, he was pretty serious about it, but there was a real buzz around the school. Little groups huddled in corners whispering to one another and staring suspiciously at any passing 6th-former. Poor Sam was even hauled up in front of the head for using his asthma inhaler. Didn't tell Cills about what I'd said to the reporter. Maybe one day I'll show her this diary and she'll appreciate my genius.

Sunday 10th March Boring weekend. No good films on, invasion of Susie's 'bestest' friends. Tried watching Sky Sports on TV non-stop, but got fed up. Maybe I'll try some cannabis after all.

Tuesday 12th March Two men in faded blue jeans, who'd been hanging around the school for the last couple of days looking like sex maniacs, local flashers, or drug dealers, were actually policemen from the drugs squad. Had to miss biology for their talk. Worth it though. Scared me shitless, as they probably intended.

They started by saying there is no single reason why teenagers take drugs. Most of us will be offered them at some time or other, probably at parties or in a pub, usually by someone we know, and most of us will say 'no'. But some will try them, from curiosity, boredom or because friends are doing it. Here are the facts they gave us.

The police can stop and search anyone they suspect of carrying drugs. In the United Kingdom last year there were about 128,000 drug offenders (90% male) of whom 60,000 were cautioned and the rest sentenced in court. The maximum prison sentence for supplying other people with heroin, cocaine or lysergic acid (LSD) is 'life', and for 'using' any of these drugs – 7 years. The maximum prison sentence for 'supplying' other people with cannabis is 7 years. The police will not now prosecute you for possession of small amounts of cannabis, unless you keep on being discovered with it.

With a bit of luck, 'Spliffy' Smith might get put away for 7 years. (Wonder if you can take your A and AS levels in prison?)

The drug police then explained that when people talk about drugs, they might mean drugs which are medicines and help you – like penicillin, insulin and paracetamol. But even medicines have to be used properly. If you take too much of a medicine, or the wrong kind, this can be harmful, and they gave insulin as an example. People with diabetes, when their body doesn't make enough insulin, get sick because the amount of sugar in their blood gets really high. They have to inject themselves with artificial insulin, but if they inject too much, then the sugar in their blood gets too low and they can pass out, because the brain needs some sugar from the blood to keep it going.

However, lots of drugs AREN'T medicines – these are the illegal ones which you get arrested for if you take them. These can do harm, and with some of them, once you start taking them, it is very difficult to stop cos you get addicted (reckon this is the same as Dad being addicted to his tobacco habit).

They made us write down all the reasons we could think of why any of us would want to take illegal drugs. I think I must be a natural addict as I got the longest list:

» to feel big and hard

» to feel excited about doing something illegal

» to know what it's like

» to be like other people who are taking drugs

» to rebel and be different from everyone else

» to get my friends to admire me

» to upset my parents

» to forget about my problems, like not knowing how to tell Cills I fancy her

» to relax me so I can tell Cills I fancy her

» cos it's fun.

The police stared at my list for so long, I was convinced they thought I was already on every illegal drug there was, but finally they gave it back with a hard look.

They gave us this leaflet called 'Know Your Drug Scene', and said to look up all about drugs on a website called www.doctorann.org, as it was better to have at least some idea of what you were getting into if you were using illegal stuff. Here's some of the stuff from the leaflet.

Cannabis

So what is all this cannabis stuff?

Cannabis comes from the hemp plant. It contains something called THC (tetrahydrocannabinols) which is the chemical that has the effect.

It has more names than most people have had hot dinners, including dope, pot, weed, grass, green, hash, marijuana, blow, draw, rocky, black, leb, gear, puff.

It normally either looks like dried-up grass, or comes in a hard block. It is usually smoked but can also be eaten.

What happens when you take it?

If you smoke cannabis, it starts having an effect after a few minutes and the effects can last up to 3 hours. But if you have a bad time with it, it can take much longer to wear off. It can have very different effects on different people:

» you may feel great – happy, relaxed, talkative and giggly

» you may feel as if you are much more aware of what's going on around you

» you may feel anxious, confused, withdrawn, depressed, and that everyone is getting at you

» you may feel a combination of these things.

So why all the fuss?

If you use a lot:

» you begin to...oh, yeah...sort of...um...forget things

» you lose your, what's it called? That thing...um, er...concentration

» this can give you trouble with your schoolwork and your social life

>> in fact, you can become a real 'druggie'.

OK, so that doesn't sound so bad

Well – there's more. If you tend to get a bit depressed or anxious anyhow, then there are forms of cannabis – one called skunk because it stinks and another called 'chaos' for obvious reasons – which make you sleepless, bad-tempered, and not nice to know at all. And beware, a small number of vulnerable people can go really funny when they smoke cannabis, and it can even bring on a mental illness.

And the real problem?

The police – at present it is illegal to possess cannabis or to supply it. If you're found with it, you may just get a caution and the police will not normally prosecute you for possessing a small amount, though you can get up to 7 years for supplying.

In fact, the majority of people in Great Britain on drug charges are there because of cannabis. Most people don't know that.

WHAT YOU MAY ALSO GET IS A POLICE RECORD WHICH CERTAINLY WON'T HELP YOUR CHANCES OF GETTING A JOB OR GOING ABROAD.

I asked the policemen why they smoked fags, and they admitted it was just as well one habit didn't always lead to another or they'd be on the big H by now. I'm still determined not to get hooked on even nicotine. Perhaps I can get some money out of Dad for not smoking, like Sam's dad's promised him.

Wonder if all these facts might make someone actually want to try drugs? Doubt it though, especially after what was to come...the bad effects of other drugs.

The leaflet goes on to say that drugs like **amphetamines**, which are also called speed, uppers, whizz and billy (crazy names), can stop you sleeping. They make you restless, they make you sweat, feel dizzy and very anxious, and then you collapse exhausted and feeling depressed.

Ecstasy did not sound ecstatic to me. Was mainly used at rave parties way back in the 90s, as it made the music sound better and people were able to dance longer, but about 50 people in the UK have died when using it. Nobody knows exactly how much damage it can cause, but there are more and more real worries about it harming your brain. (So it would probably be OK if Susie took some as she doesn't have a brain to start with.)

The leaflet said that the real nasties are heroin, cocaine, and some sort of chemical alternative called '**crack**' – which is the worst for getting addicted. **Heroin** is also called junk, H, gear, smack or brown. People using it regularly get called 'the living dead', with shakes, cramps and tiredness. All these drugs can give you real trouble.

Glue-sniffing and other solvent abuse can sometimes lead to getting infections in your chest and other things like liver and kidney damage. People who sniff glue get red marks around the nose and sores around the mouth. The main danger, though, is being right stupid and falling off a building or under a car, or drowning, while under the effects of the stuff. Sometimes sniffing butane gas, which is put into lighters, can make you drop down dead.

Using **cocaine** can lead to depression, mashes up the inside of your nose, and causes paranoia. (Had to look that one up. Means 'You think everyone hates you'. I have that problem all the time, except I don't think it, I know it.)

After reading all this, had to sit next to the 100-kilo blancmange – 'Guzzler Guts' Gary – at lunch. He's definitely addicted, and not only to food as it turned out. He loosened his mouth and his belt and revealed all, with half the school listening in.

'*The first time I had a sniff of globby glue,*' another huge greasy sausage sank between his mighty yellow fangs, '*was with these kids in a multi-storey car park near the local supermarket. I'd already been sniffing gas for a couple of months, so was used to the dizziness and all that, but I kept on blowing in the bag until I blacked out on the floor.'* I'm surprised the car park didn't fall down.

'While I was sniffing, I could see all these creatures and ghosts coming out of the walls and things attacking me. When you first sniff glue, there are a few things that can happen. You can drop down dead, be happy or very unhappy. For me – well, I got depressed. Can't remember why cos I was so high on the glue. At the time I really felt like killing myself, then I got used to it and felt good. When I first started, I worried about it a lot. Then I got ill with tummy pains and started coughing up blood. The only dangerous thing that happened to me was that I was in this park, and was higher than high, and needed some more glue, so I ran across the road to the glue shop and nearly got mowed down by a bus.' Said I wondered if the bus knew what a lucky escape it had!

Anyhow this Gary character has kicked the habit, and thinks there ought to be a law against selling glue to children. Told him he'd gone from glue to grub to greediness to grossness cos of his need for 'oral gratification'. Had to explain this meant he liked 'stuffing his face'. He said he could've told me that, so why did I have to use such long words?

Wednesday 13th March Poured with rain. The 'faded jeans' sex maniacs, alias the drugs police, have disappeared from the school gates, so the girls have stopped hanging out there too.

Friday 15th March Mum's in a real 'why's everybody getting at me' mood. Been out every night doing her 'good deeds for the neighborhood' act. Rest of us had council of war over how to get her to go to bed – one thing she refuses to do when she's wiped out, as she prefers to drag herself around and be moody with us all instead. Dad found her asleep in the bath covered with soggy pages of 'Good Housekeeping' magazine. She's got awful reading habits but at least she won't need her sleeping tablets tonight.

Couldn't resist getting my own back. I told Mum how Miss 'Big Arse' Court, our sports teacher, didn't think lying in baths was any good for stress and that Mum should be out doing something active like aerobics, which would get her 'natural endorphins' working. Got told off for using 'bad language' – if parents were any more stupid, you'd have to water them twice a week.

Has **Susie** Started **Yet?**

Saturday 16th March Real find – but I hope nobody reads THIS! Susie's out this morning buying new clothes again with Mum, after moaning about wearing Sally's cast-offs. All she wants these days is to be sorted like her friends. Was desperately looking for my only clean T-shirt, mottoed 'WHY SHOULD I TIDY MY ROOM WHEN THE WORLD'S IN SUCH A MESS?' All my others were dirty and stuffed down the side of my bed cos as usual I'd forgotten to give them to Mum to wash. Eventually found it in Susie's bottom drawer, PLUS HER DIARY! Didn't mean to read it but sort of fell open in my hands. Covers all the stuff that I hadn't been picking up from snooping in her emails – a real treat…

Tuesday 19th February

Went to Kate's house for the night.

Wednesday 20th February

Bov's out all the time. Seems to be with a new tom every night. Dad's fed up with all the smell they make.

Aaargghh! This was really boring. Don't know why girls bother to keep a diary about this sort of thing. I thought it would be all about Kate going through her development and things…

Thursday 21ˢᵗ February

Kate says she fancies Pete. I told her he picks his nose in the bath.

Aha! This was more like it…but Kate…interested in me? Well, I can see why, but she hardly has tits, and anyhow it's a lie cos I don't pick my nose in the bath – do it in the lav instead.

Friday 22ⁿᵈ February

Hope Mum and Dad aren't getting divorced. They've had a terrible row. It's all Pete's fault, getting at me as usual. Sally says it's all going to be all right, but I'm not so sure.

Tuesday 26ᵗʰ February

At school today Dave, a real minger who wears track suits, asked Kate if she'd started her periods yet. She went red and said it was none of his business. Don't know why boys should be interested anyhow. Later she told me she had started and that was why she wouldn't go swimming with me last week. Was really miffed that she hadn't told me before.

Kate said they started 2 months ago. She had been staying at her gran's and had had a tummy ache and gone to bed early. In the morning she'd woken up and thought that she'd wet the bed. But it was just a little blood. She'd felt sooooo embarrassed and didn't know what to do with the sheets, but her gran was really nice.

Kate's mum had told her all about it and so she had really wanted to start her periods, but now she had, she felt a bit annoyed. Though she was also glad to have joined the other girls who had started in the same year – definitely made ME feel left out. Anyhow her gran had bought some sanitary towels as she didn't have any in the house – her periods had stopped years ago.

Her gran had said that when she was young nobody had told her anything. They called periods the 'curse' and their 'monthlies' and thought they were dirty, and for some reason when they had one weren't even allowed to wash their hair. She had had to wear an awful elastic belt thing to keep a thick towel in place, which felt a bit like wearing a mattress. But luckily she knew that today they have very comfortable, slim 'press on' ones – the very latest style. Kate's mum had also told her all about tampons, and said that it would be perfectly OK to use them, especially if she wanted to go swimming, but Kate wasn't sure she wanted to try them yet.

Kate's lent me a book her mum had got her called 'Have You Started Yet?' It's good and has lots of people's points of view in it, and tells you in a simple way exactly what happens and how. Reckon I might get embarrassed talking about periods, but reading about them is fine. I don't know what it'll be like for me. I'm not really scared. I suppose it's just part of growing up. It's funny to think that some of my friends can have babies already. Really strange.

Couldn't find my new pink socks this evening – wonder if Pete's borrowed them, but pink's not his colour.

Friday 1st March

Left my homework at school. Watched a really good programme on pets. Wonder if Bovril might have kittens? Still seems to be a bit of a kitten herself.

Saturday 2nd March

Mum's got no idea. Was out shopping and got soaked, so she made me take off all my wet things, including knickers, in the kitchen and run upstairs naked to the bath. I don't think she sees that I might be embarrassed, just because SHE goes around starkers all the time.

On the way upstairs Mum asked about the lumps on my chest. I'm not really embarrassed by them, but I certainly don't like to be seen with nothing on. My breasts are still very small and hurt a bit when I run. I've got some hair too. Mum suggested I get a bra, but I told her it was blindingly obvious I've nothing to put in one. I hope they never get as big as Sally's. When she just has a T-shirt on, Pete calls her 'wobbly'. When mine first started to appear, I got dead scared. I didn't see myself as that old, but I've got used to it now. Strange to think there's no going back to being a child.

Didn't know that girls get breasts before they start their periods. My changes somehow seem less obvious – like my voice changing. Aunty Pam phoned the other day and started a long conversation about Uncle Bob's operation, thinking I was Dad.

Sunday 3rd March

Have read some more of 'Have You Started Yet?' Pete always seemed to be around just when I was going to talk to Mum about my periods. But Mum got the message, and when we went to visit Uncle Bob in hospital, she suggested that Pete should stay behind and catch up with his homework, which was all about this genome project thing. Pete seemed really interested and said it would be useful when I had babies because they could have their genes changed so that they had none of my bad points. Said I wish I could change his genes so I could have a different brother.

When Mum and I were alone, I asked her when I was likely to start my periods as my breasts were beginning to grow. My book said that most girls begin between the ages of 9 and 17. Mum told me that some girls get their periods almost as soon as their breasts appear, and others got them later, but both were normal. She told me that at first I shouldn't expect my periods to happen every month. I might have just a few spots of blood and then nothing for a bit. When they settled down, the amount of blood I would lose would be about a third of a mugful each time. Though most women get periods every month, a few women get them every 3 weeks, and a few every 6 weeks. Also, the time a period lasts is different and is between 1 or 2 days and a week. Mum said she'd get me a packet of sanitary towels just to be prepared.

At the hospital we gave Uncle Bob the flowers we had got and he was really embarrassing. 'I bet you have all the boys chasing after you, because you're becoming a real woman now, aren't you?' I wasn't going to tell HIM I haven't started yet!

Monday 4th March

Some more time for reading this evening. Funny to think there are 200,000 little eggs sitting around in my ovaries. Even though over my whole lifetime, only 400 or so will ever get released – awful waste. Every month, hormone messages from my brain will tell my ovaries to release an egg. If the egg doesn't meet a sperm and get fertilized, then whoosh, out of my vagina it comes, along with the cells and blood from the lining of my uterus – rather like flushing the loo. Certainly don't want a boy's sperm near me when I am a teenager, thanks very much. I reckon I don't want babies till I am at least 25 and with a good job so I can look after myself.

Kate reckons there should be a button you can press so it could all come out at once, instead of messily dribbling out over several days, and thinks tampons and sanitary towels should be free on the National Health Service. What's also clever is the way the brain sends different hormone messages when you get pregnant, so that you don't have a period and the lining of your uterus stays all ready for the fertilized egg to start growing there into a baby.

Tuesday 5th March

Had a stomach ache today. Kept rushing to the loo to see if I'd started, especially as I felt a bit wet down there. It was nothing except a bit of what the book calls 'normal vaginal discharge'. Sometimes this happens before you have a period, so it might be going to happen to me soon. Hope so. Just don't let it happen when I go swimming.

Fed up with all the old clothes I have to wear. Make me look totally babyish.

Wednesday 6th March

The stomach ache turned out to be the diarrhoea squits. Must have caught it from Jane, who was off school with the same thing. Pete's his usual awful self. 'Ugh! Don't come near me with your dirty germs. Hope you've washed your hands after the loo. That's how these things get spread, you know — reckon you should be put down like all those sheep with foot and mouth'. Mum told me not to eat and just have lots of drinks of water and coke until my insides had recovered and could cope with food again. Now I'm starving.

Missed all the drama at school about drugs.

Thursday 7th March

Mum's all touchy and mouchy. Perhaps she's got PMT like I read about in the book. Pete thought PMT stood for Pre-Menstrual Tantrums. Could see what he meant, but he's such a 'know-all', I didn't put him right.

I'm sure it means Pre-Menstrual Tantrums. It must be Susie who's wrong. I'll have to look it up.

Friday 8th March

Mum's just got the squits like me. Heard her going to the loo all night. Hope she's better tomorrow so we can go shopping.

Saturday 9th March

Only got lovely new red and blue swimsuit from Top Shop as Mum's a bit short of money this week and didn't have the energy to go round many shops. Hate those changing rooms where you are all together – seemed like everyone was looking at me. Tried it on without taking my shirt off; and with Mum telling me not to

be silly, we're all the same. Looking around, we jolly well aren't. Liz has tiny breasts and huge nipples. Her new bikini emphasizes her Egyptian look. The boys all call her 'pyramid', and say things like she would have to sleep on her back on a water bed or she'd puncture it. She's very tall and said that she wishes her pituitary gland would concentrate on making her grow out frontwards rather than upwards. Still, according to Kate, she spent all her time hanging about the school gates when the drug policemen were there, so her hormones must be doing something.

Sunday 10th March

Uncle Bob's out of hospital, and Mum and Dad have gone off to visit. Couldn't face any more of his embarrassing remarks myself. Wandered into Sally's room to try on one of her bras, but she was there. She started to tease me about not starting yet.

She said that before she started she was jealous of all her friends who had. Her best friend had told her about it, like it was some incredible secret and terribly exciting. Another of her friends had really bad period pains, and if Sally was nasty to her at all, she looked at her pityingly and said, 'Look, when you're a woman you'll understand the pain and anguish it causes.' Sally said, 'A woman! She was only 13.'

When Sally had started, it was just after a biology lesson, and she was a bit alarmed but also excited. She was too embarrassed to tell any of her friends, because when she thought about it, it seemed a pretty foul idea. It didn't cause her any trouble at first, no tummy pains or PMT or anything, but later she started getting occasional tummy cramps with her periods and took paracetamol, which helped. Now the doctor gives her some tablets, because the cramps are worse and she has this swollen feeling.

Sally told me how to use tampons, which was just as well because I couldn't see how I would ever get them in. She said she had found them difficult, and hadn't put them far enough up because she thought they would get lost inside. Then she'd discovered that there are two kinds of tampon. Some have applicators – shiny white cardboard tubes around them. These slip in easily. You then pull out the cardboard, leaving the tampon in the right place in your vagina. The others don't have applicators. You just have to push them in until they feel comfortable. Both kinds come with a diagram showing how to use them. And both have a thread attached to the bottom of the tampon, to pull it out with.

I was just finishing when the front door slammed and Mum shouted 'Pete' up the stairs, so I stuffed the diary back, blushing like mad. Back to picking my nose in the bog.

6 My Own **'Changes'**
Start, but They Take
a Loooong Time

Sunday 17th March With me snooping in Susie's email and reading her diary, reckon I'll have to be careful what I say in front of her or she'll wonder how I know some things, but real glad I don't have to have periods. Wish that my voice breaking just happened overnight, though. For months now I'm not sure what's going to come out of my mouth – foghorn or squeak.

My own changes must be obvious to everyone cos Dad keeps trying to bring up the subject of 'puberty' and 'the facts of life'. Must've been him that left the book about sex and stuff in my room. This morning he started to tell me about what he called 'the birds and the bees', so I told him I knew it all already – to help him out, as I began to feel as embarrassed as him. He looked relieved and rushed off to the garage to have a fag in secret. I really feel for Dad sometimes. I wonder if Mum's behind all this? I'd have thought she had enough to worry about, what with Susie's changes. Don't know why grown-ups want to talk about these things all the time. They must be sex mad.

Monday 18th March Went with Dad to see Uncle Bob this evening – seems to be surviving OK. I reckon he must have a one-track mind too. His first words were, 'Got yourself a girlfriend yet then?', and he promised me a razor for my next birthday. I'd rather have the money. But what even Dad embarrassingly refers to as 'your moustache' is definitely going to need a scrape soon. The hairs under my arms, and around my dick, haven't been slow in growing either, but I don't worry about them – I just wear long shirts. Problem is that I'm still very short in height.

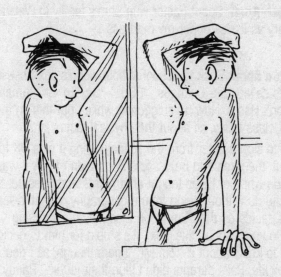

Haven't talked to anyone about it all, except jokingly with my friends. Gets a bit mean sometimes, like James saying that Randy Joe thought he'd grown a pubic hair till he discovered it was his dick. Suppose we're all going through it together, though we're too embarrassed to talk about it. Somehow, being 'inside' myself makes me feel completely different about my own changes than about my friends' changes.

Thursday 28th March Tried to find Susie's diary again. It's not in her drawer. Wonder if she guessed? Knowing her, she's probably dusted it for fingerprints.

Friday 5th April Cat's out of the bag! After school Susie disappeared. At supper she gave us all meaningful looks and announced she'd bought a diary with a lock on. Mum suggested she could look after the spare key if Susie wanted, and then suddenly went bright red. Saved!

Tuesday 9th April Have taken to hiding MY diary under my mattress…don't trust Mum for a second.

Tuesday 16th April Spent Easter with Sam's family in Wales. Forgot to take my diary as it was under my mattress.

Monday 22nd April Back to school. Whole world's sex-obsessed, though at school it's called 'Life Changes', 'PSHE', 'Sex Ed' or 'Human Reproduction'. Had a 'Now no sniggering while I put this on the blackboard' class today, all about the physical facts.

Dad had to sign a letter from the school saying it was OK for me to be taught about 'the birds and bees'. Told Dad I didn't think it was right for him to decide whether I was taught about birds and bees, let alone sex… After all, I can do without being taught geography or maths – he's welcome to decide on that. But when it comes to something I really want (and need) to know about, like 'sex', it's stupid for him to decide. Not sure I want to know about it from Mr Rogers though, as I doubt whether he has a sex life. Raj's parents didn't sign their letter – Randy Joe teased Raj that he wouldn't know where to put it when he grows up. Bit mean as his parents don't want him being taught on religious grounds. I'm lending him my book.

Turns out that boys' puberty tends to start between the ages of 10 and 13, and finishes at any time up to 18. There's still time for me then, as I'm shorter than many of my friends. Even the girls are taller, but apparently on average they start their changes 2 years ahead of us boys.

In boys, the first thing is our balls get bigger, and over 3 years they increase 7 times in size. Next comes pubic hair, and bits of hair under our arms, and with some of us hair on our chests too. Hope I don't get hair on my chest. Wonder if anyone shaves there? Then our height goes shooting up – can't be too soon for me. We grow a quarter of our final height during this time. Then our penis grows in length. Keep on measuring mine.

All these things start at different times in different boys, go on for different lengths of time, and occur in different orders. In one way, we all end up the same after we've been through puberty, but in another we all end up different, because we still have different sizes and shapes and looks.

Lots of other changes are going on too – muscles getting bigger and heavier, shoulders broader, voices deeper because of bigger vocal cords. Like Susie's changes, all these things in boys are controlled by chemicals called hormones produced in our brains – but it's the testosterone doing it for me and my mates.

The diagrams and description of male parts and an erection on the board made it all look totally unreal – a bit like a bike tyre being pumped up. It seems there are muscles inside our dicks which stop the blood flowing out, but which go on letting the blood flow in. More and more blood fills it up, making it bigger and bigger and longer and longer.

Were also taught how vulnerable our poor old sperm is and what a short life it has. That's why we have to make about 60,000,000 sperms in the 3 millilitres of fluid that come out each time we make love or masturbate – that's just under a teaspoonful. Only one of these spermies is needed to fertilize an egg, though. What a fantastic waste. It's funny how difficult it is to connect all this with my own body. Mr Rogers, of 'Sex Ed' fame, said this was only the physical side of things, and he'd talk about 'feelings', about sex and love next lesson on Friday – think I'm going to get sick.

Tuesday 23rd April If we have greasy chips and hamburgers one more time for school lunch, I'll definitely get mad cow disease (or get Mum to make me packed lunches). The sex obsession goes on. I scored by bringing in the book Dad's given me. Everyone pretended not to be interested, but then all looked at the bit on 'Normal Size of Penises'. It said:

The majority of boys and men think that their penis is too small and it is very difficult sometimes to convince them otherwise. So an American doctor has done some research, using a ruler to measure the length of the non-erect penis of boys and men of different ages.

AGE	RANGE OF PENILE LENGTH
10	4 to 8 cm
12	5 to 10 cm
14	6 to 14 cm
16	10 to 15 cm
18	11 to 17 cm

For most men and boys it was found that, however small the non-erect penis was, penises were all roughly the same length when erect.

Mine goes straight from a floppy start of 11.2 cms to a standing finish of 15.4 cms in 30 seconds Obviously hasn't reached its maximum acceleration or length yet. I wonder what I'd get an Olympic gold medal for?

Wednesday 24th April Bit of a sore throat today, so looked pathetic and told Mum. Usual sympathy from her, which meant taking my temperature, finding it normal, giving me two paracetamol and ordering me to school. Threw up all over the floor in class and got sent home. Hope this made Mum feel really guilty.

Thursday 25th April Typical – now Mum's convinced I'm really ill. Though still wouldn't call the doctor. Said it was probably a viral infection. As I had a headache, Sam said I should check for a rash that didn't fade when you pressed a glass against it – could be meningitis. He knows all this stuff cos of his dad. Mum said not to worry, I wasn't that ill, and certainly there's no rash. Had to spend a boring day in bed though.

Felt OK by evening but not allowed to go out. May not be meningitis, but think I'm getting pimples on my nose. Bovril's had her kittens in the dirty clothes under my bed. Susie's furious cos she missed seeing them come out. Spent evening searching for girlie stuff on my computer, but unlike the rest of the world couldn't find any. And Susie kept walking in unannounced – in order to see the kittens.

Friday 26th April Back to school, and it turned out the talk on 'Feelings' was just a film called *Personal Relationships*. Typical grown-ups' views on what they think we're thinking. Managed to get some of it right though. It tried to say that at our age we tend to:

» lose interest in things that our parents organize for us, and are more reluctant to accept advice and criticism (just like Susie, in fact).

» feel concerned about, but also uncertain about, our appearance and whether we are attractive in other people's eyes (this applies to me).

» have times when we feel totally bored, unwanted by everyone, and have nothing to do, when everyone else seems to be having a really good time (too right).

» feel good about the world one day and totally upset by it the next.

» worry about whether we are ever going to get to know a girlfriend or boyfriend really well (like Cills and me).

» think we are different from everyone else, but at the same time desperately want to be the same.

» worry whether our sexual feelings are normal. (Are they too strong or too weak? Are we gay? Should we be worrying about masturbation, wet dreams, the size of our penises, our breasts, and when our periods are going to start?)

In the discussion afterwards I said I didn't think that we WERE all that interested in ourselves, and it seemed it was the grown-ups who were more interested than us. Obvious from the questions some of my friends asked that they don't even know what wet dreams are.

Mr Rogers said that people vary in their interest in sex, and whether they felt attracted to people of the opposite sex or the same sex, and all are normal. Then he explained that wet dreams are sexy dreams during which you ejaculate or 'come' while still asleep. They are called 'wet' dreams because you wet the bed with your sperm. He went on to explain that boys and girls find that masturbation is 'a harmless and very pleasant way of relieving feelings of sexual tension' and that you aren't oversexed if you do masturbate, wank, pull yourself off, beat your salami, toss off, or whatever else you call it, and you aren't undersexed if you don't.

What was really good was that Mr Rogers was not at all embarrassed when talking about these things. Amazing to think that EVERY person that one EVER sees is the result of two people making love and a sperm fertilizing an egg – even Mr Rogers! Looked at everyone in school with new eyes. I wonder if Mum and Dad still do it – ugh.

Tuesday 30th April Caught out by Mum again. After my bike accident, she'd bought me really gross black-leather school shoes to wear, instead of my ruined white trainers. Been outsmarting her by changing into the trainers in the garage on the way to school. Got back today to change into Mum's shoes and found them with a note saying, 'Wear them at school or there's no pocket money,' signed 'Your Mother'. I know she'll forget, and with luck I'll be able to wear my old trainers and have my pocket money as well. She's really safe sometimes.

Friday 3rd May Was right – Mum's forgotten. Cycled to school in my trainers. Decided to ask Cills if she'd come to the cinema on Sunday.

Saturday 4th May Cills is already going with Randy Joe. Feel a complete failure.

7

Learning to **Live** with my **Zits**

Tuesday 7th May Worse and worser – pimples are turning into massive spots. Every time I look, another has appeared. My skin's gone all greasy, with lumps around my nose – disgusting. Dad's sympathetic, but not much help. Said, 'Oh, it's just acne. Everyone gets it when they're teenagers'. JUST! That's no help to someone with a face covered in pussy molehills. He went on about how they'd clear up soon, but they haven't gone yet and it's 3 days already. Tried squeezing them, and although got something out, it's made them worse! Some seem to have black heads, others have white heads. Maybe it's cos I don't wash enough.

Wednesday 8th May A black(head) day in my life. In school Cills said, 'Ugh, what have you done to your face?' I thought that would have been blindingly obvious. She wears so much make-up, you'd need a spade to find out what's happening underneath. Anyhow, I know that what she really worries about is being too hairy, so called her 'ape face'. You've heard about 'road' rage – well, you ain't seen nothing till you've seen 'Cills' rage.

Thursday 9th May Aaarggghhh, they're spreading! Slogs was kind enough to point it out to me after games today. Said my back looked like a pizza. Checked in the mirror. He's right. Where are they going to spread to next – my bum?

Friday 10th May Good old Mum – thought she hadn't noticed. She's left a tube of cream in my room, plus an article she'd found in an old Sunday colour supplement. It's called 'A Spot of Bother' and seems to know what it's talking about.

'Acne happens most commonly in young people because of the surge in hormones that comes with puberty. It tends to be worse in boys and affects the face and shoulders most, because that's where hair follicles are commonest.

There are a lot of myths about what causes acne. It isn't caused by eating too much sugar or chips; or by masturbation. (Relieved about that, as I had begun to think that was why me and most of my friends had zits.) Nor do people get acne because they don't wash enough. Washing your face twice a day with soap and water should help in most cases, especially if you use a medicated soap that contains an antiseptic. However, these soaps will help only mild cases, and you need to use them for several weeks.

Some shampoos, foundation creams, moisturizers and hair conditioners can make acne worse – particularly those which are heavy and greasy. (Will pass some of this on to Cills.)

Eye make-up, lipstick, powders, blushers and toilet waters, on the other hand, shouldn't cause you any problems. (Don't use them myself).

One thing that you can try for yourself to help your acne is to go out in the sun. Sunlight is usually good for spots. It reduces the number of bacteria in the skin, encourages peeling (ugh) to get rid of the horny layer of skin, loosens blackheads, and decreases the rate at which sebum is produced...'

Still don't really understand why I've got them, or what 'sebum' is, but DOES NOT sound nice.

Saturday 11th May Aunty Pam's coming tomorrow! Horrible. Maybe she won't kiss me cos of my acne. Only advantage I can think of. Put the cream on for the second time today. Amazed there's no improvement.

Mum and Dad went out for an hour, leaving me to 'baby-sit' for Susie, which she hates. Told her she *is* still a baby, as she spends all her time making clothes for her Barbie doll. She'll begin to look like one of them soon, but without the tits. Tried persuading Mum and Dad to pay me. They refused with an argument about how they didn't make me pay for my meals. Offered to go and eat at McDonald's if that was their problem.

Sunday 12th May Aunty Pam came and gave me the kiss of Dracula, despite my zits. Hope they ARE catching. Wonder where I can find out more about acne? Might try the www.doctorann.org site again. Can't understand it – the Americans have Star Wars defence systems which can hit rockets a million miles away but they can't cure acne – disaster. Perhaps the genome project will sort out acne? Sam's Dad will know.

Monday 13th May Dictionary not much help. Said acne was a 'skin eruption with red pimples'. Makes my face sound like a volcano. In despair about the cream I'm using. Seems a complete waste of time, but www.doctorann.org website said it's worth trying different creams and lotions till you find one that works on your particular skin. Mum's got me this new lotion. Says it's cheaper, and the chemist told her there is nothing to show that more expensive creams work better. Just need to try one after the other for a bit to find out which one works.

Rushed up to the bathroom to use it, as school party is in only 2 weeks' time and I'm getting desperado. Embarrassing enough asking a girl to dance, let alone if you've got acne from your bum upwards! Lotion stung when I put it on, so looked at the instructions to make sure I was doing it right. There was a long leaflet giving all the facts.

Apparently 70% of the teenage population have acne at one time or another. It's not a disease but just a normal part of growing up. Thanks a lot, that makes all the difference!

It usually disappears between the ages of 16 and 25. You can get acne anywhere you have hairs (ANYWHERE? I hope not) because it is in the hair follicles that it starts, but it mainly affects the face, back, shoulders and chest (what a relief).

It isn't catching – so much for my revenge on Aunty Pam – and my fantasies about kissing a girl can live on.

'Sebum' is a substance secreted by the sebaceous glands, next to the hair follicles. Apparently a normal amount of sebum helps keep the skin slightly oily and protects it from wetness, bacteria and other things, but too much gives the skin the greasiness I find so gross.

Some girls have acne worse at the times of their periods. (At least I don't have that trouble.)

It's easier to use an electric razor with acne than to shave with soap. (Will Dad let me use his?)

Washing with an antiseptic soap helps. (Must get Mum to get me some of that as well.)

It's better not to squeeze spots because they tend to get infected and you may end up with more. But if you do have to fiddle with them (who doesn't?), make sure your hands are clean and only squeeze the blackheads. It even explained why blackheads are black. Apparently it's nothing to do with dirt – just a bit of pigment from the skin.

At the end it said, 'Most mild acne clears either without treatment or after using a cream or lotion. If it doesn't, it is best to consult your family doctor, who can prescribe other treatments.'

While reading all this, kept looking in the mirror to see if the lotion was working. Then noticed leaflet said that it may take several days to work. Went to bed.

Friday 24th May Even Susie has noticed my zits are better. Just as well, as it's the school party thing tonight. I've nearly forgotten what I look like without spots. Don't think my friends would recognize me if all the zits disappeared. Anyway, I'll keep on with the soap just in case. Today noticed that even Randy Joe has a few zits. Doesn't seem to have put his girlies off though. Maybe cos most of them have spots too.

Went to school do. Turned out to be too dark to have to worry about how we looked. Danced once with Cills – tried a fumble but didn't get anywhere. Still a determined virgin but it'll take more than that to put me off. She's had her nose pierced to match her tummy button – what next?

8

Sal's
Sex Life
Goes
Wrong

Saturday 25th May No sleep last night – overheating after body contact with Cills. Incredibly annoying, especially when I am overtired anyhow and it seems to come in runs of a few nights at a time. Worry that I'm not getting all the sleep I need, and am going to be tired and grumpy and no good at anything next day. Tried relaxing, reading my old books (new books make me too excited) and counting Cills jumping over fences, but all I think about is her body and how I'm never going to get to sleep, and so I don't.

Mum reckons I don't get enough exercise. I read somewhere that having sex is exercise equivalent to running a mile. Don't think my own efforts on myself demand the same energy, but at least this way I won't lose sleep worrying what nasty sexually transmitted diseases I might be getting – like Aids.

Finally thought I'd go and get a hot drink. Was around midnight and everyone should've been in bed. About to go into the kitchen when I heard Mum and Sally behind the door. Sally was sobbing like a drain, saying she thought she might be pregnant. WHAAAAAAT! I couldn't believe my ears – someone had scored with my sister! My ear found itself glued to the door and just wouldn't come away.

MUM: Here, have a hanky. For God's sake, haven't you been using something, after all we talked about?

SAL: Didn't think anything was going to happen, did I? We were at a party last week and we'd been drinking. It only happened once, and I wasn't going to take the Pill for months and months, on the off chance something might happen, was I? Anyway, if I had been taking it, Mike might have thought I was easy.

MUM: Why didn't you ask him to use something then? It was just as much his responsibility as yours, and anyhow what about infections? Did you think about that?

SAL: Couldn't suddenly stop half-way through and ask him, could I?

MUM: You bloody well could have and should have. Or you should have got emergency contraception – you know that. You could have gone to any doctor and you can use it up to 3 days afterwards. However, it's a bit late for that now.

SAL: What are we going to do? Please, please don't tell Dad. He'll be mad at me and I feel right stupid enough already.

MUM: We? OK, I'm with you here. Best thing is for us to go to the doctor's Monday, and then we'll...

Gave up on my hot drink at this point and bolted upstairs. Can see why they're discussing putting condom machines in the 6th-form toilets at school. Was now more insomniac than ever, but insomnia was a minor problem compared with Sal's. Tried reading Harry P. again and ... zzzzzzzzzzzzzzzzzzzzzzzzzzz.

9

Susie Gets **Hayfever**

Monday 27th May Susie's even more revolting than usual. Her sniffling sounds like a foot-and-mouth pig with indigestion. Said I'd have my breakfast in the other room cos I couldn't stand it any longer. So Susie screamed and burst into tears, while Mum made a face at me for being unsympathetic. No one amused when I said it was like sitting next to a vacuum cleaner gone wrong. Couldn't stop thinking about all that yukky green snot being sucked down the back of her throat.

Wednesday 29th May Susie's still sniffing. Hope I don't catch it. Bovril's no longer feeding her kittens, and is off playing with the toms again. Sally's not having a baby and she's bust up with Mike – official (via the kitchen door) – and making Mum really cross cos she's out clubbing when she should be revising.

Thursday 30th May Now it's Susie's sneezing, snoring and sniffling all night that's stopping me sleeping. No toilet paper in the bog cos Susie's room and the rest of the house are covered with a snow layer of crumpled white toilet tissues. Reckon it's better than her sniffing though. Sally says she bets it's not a cold, but hayfever, like she gets herself sometimes. Whatever it is, I still hope I don't catch it.

Saturday 1st June Brilliant sunny day. Persuaded on to tennis court by Sam, who said it would be good for me. Susie flopping around the house looking red-eyed, as if she's been crying all night, and says she's got a horrible headache. Murdered by Sam of course cos he's brilliant at everything – next thing he'll be playing at Wimbledon.

Had my weekly bath (under threat of no pocket money from Mum) and was listening to the radio. There was a 'phone-in' on hayfever. Sal was right, this is what Susie has. Lots of it around at the moment, on account of the 'pollen count' being so high cos of the hot weather. This pollen is made up of seeds that come from trees and grasses during the spring and summer, specially on a hot sunny day after it's rained. The runny nose, sneezing and itchy eyes are the body's way of trying to get rid of this pollen stuff.

Got me wondering why I hadn't got it, so leapt out of my bath leaving a trail of wet footprints, with a towel round my privates to make me half-decent (wasn't having anyone seeing MY BITS, even if half the rest of my family like going around exposing themselves). Marched downstairs to the phone, my stomach in my mouth from nerves. But had to find out, and suddenly there I was on the radio, hoping that at least one of my friends (if I have any) was listening to my radio stardom so that they could broadcast the fact in school Monday.

'Is hayfever catching', I wanted to know, 'and how come I don't have it?' Madam Clever Doc on the other end of the line put on her poshest medical voice: *'What a good question. How old are you and may we know your name?'* '18 and my name's Sam', I lied, losing my nerve. Explosive laughter from Susie who had appeared from nowhere between sneezes.

'Well, Sam, hayfever is a kind of allergy, which means that your body becomes very sensitive to certain substances. These substances, like pollens, are called allergens and when they get into your body, some of the white cells in your blood produce complicated chemical substances called antibodies to get rid of them. When the allergens and antibodies meet, they produce a reaction which brings about the release of a substance called histamine, and it's this that causes hayfever sufferers to sneeze and have runny eyes. Nobody knows why some people have this special sensitivity to things like pollens. And I thought it was me that was meant to be the sensitive one. *Usually antibodies are good things to have, as they help fight off bacteria which cause many diseases.'*

'About one in 10 people have hayfever, and although it tends to run in families, you don't catch it from someone else. Some people are born with a tendency to have it.' Couldn't waste the chance, so asked her if I could use corks to stop my sister's nose from running.

Susie hacked my ankle while the voice down the phone said, *'Well, Sam, that's another good question.'* (Mrs Smellie could learn something from her.) *'There's a wide range of things that you can do, though corking your sister's nose isn't one of them. There are medicines that you can take. It's very unfortunate that exams are often held at the same time of year as the hayfever season. If your sister's taking exams, she should go and see your own family doctor and get some treatment. If it's really bad, the doctor may even give her a note for the teacher.'* She added that this couldn't be used as an excuse for getting poor marks unless the hayfever was very bad. Decided that I wanted to hear MY voice again.

'What about my sister's nose? That's the real problem.' *'Well, if antihistamines don't help,'* she said, *'there are special sprays on prescription from your doctor, which your sister can squirt up her nose. For more information about hayfever, as well as anything you want to know about your health, you can check out two websites, www.teenagehealthfreak.org and www.Nhsdirect.com'.* Was just going to ask about some of Susie's other nasty habits when the radio presenter said, *'Well, thank you very much, Sam, and our next question comes from a Mrs Snodgrass.'*

Reckon she deserved to have hayfever with a name like that. Her question was about other kinds of treatment than those given by doctors. Apparently all sorts of things have been tried for hayfever. You can try hypnotism, acupuncture, homeopathy and other things. At the end of the programme they said to write for a special pack explaining all about hayfever. Told Susie that I'd do that for her. She looked totally surprised – it's not often that I'm helpful to my sister.

Sunday 2nd June Went to the local park for a picnic. Real hot for once – maybe global warming's not all bad, though seemed that 5 million other people had nothing better to do with their Sundays. Watched some grown-ups playing at being children with their radio-controlled, 'better than the real thing' model boats. Posers. Everything ruined by Susie feeling miserable as usual.

Mum's going to take Susie to the doctor's first thing on Monday morning. Got away with watching telly half the evening as everyone was fussing over Susie.

To take my sniffling sister's mind off her pathetic nose, I told her how in our 'sex ed' class Mr Rogers had told us about the biggest study of sex that had ever happened in Britain. It was first done some years ago and has just been redone now. She asked whether I was part of it, so I said my questionnaire had got lost in the post. Didn't tell her it would've been blank anyhow! Wasn't sure Mum would approve, but thought Susie should have the facts.

The study had shown that, although most people seem to think that

16-year-olds are all at it, in fact by 16 only 1 in 4 girls and 1 in 3 boys said that they had had sex. And many of the girls said they wished they had delayed having sex longer. This was a bit of relief for me cos hearing people talk, I think me and half my class expected to have bonked by now! Turns out that all this sex is going on in our heads, and we're just normal.

Mr Rogers had told us that most people have their first sexual experience – snogging, cuddling, petting – at around 13 years of age. (Reckon that was what I was at with Cills but didn't get far.)

One thing I didn't think Susie was old enough for was what he told us about homosexuality – boys or men fancying one another and girls or women fancying one another. The research showed that only about 6 in every 100 men and 3 in every 100 women had had a homosexual experience, but only about 1 in every 100 men and 1 in every 200 women were homosexual as adults.

This took away some of my worries, cos every time one of the 6th-form boys looked at me I was beginning to feel nervous.

Monday 3rd June Half-term, and Sally's been in charge while Mum and Dad are out working. It's not fair – when Sal 'baby-sits', she gets paid.

Instead of being her usual bossy self, Sal was actually quite nice. Turned out that she used to suffer from hayfever quite badly herself. The attacks got bad last year, when she started riding on the back of Mike's motorbike, and going out into the fields. She ignored me when I asked what they did in the fields.

To keep my end up on all this hayfever 'know how', started to tell Sal about the radio programme. She wasn't interested till I told her it was just as well she hadn't got her own motorbike yet, cos if you sneeze riding a bike at 60 miles an hour, your eyes can be closed for half a second, during which you travel 44 feet totally blind.

Tuesday 4th June Feel sorry for Susie. She's being teased at school. Her teacher said she was just putting it on, and didn't listen when Susie asked to be moved away from an open window to get away from the pollen. A friend had called her 'cry baby' when she saw her red eyes.

Susie explained that it was just hayfever, but her friend said, 'That's what they all say'. Worst was she had come fourth in the 400-metre race, all because she had felt so awful, with a streaming nose and watering eyes. Running is something she's normally CHAMPION at.

Makes me feel real angry for Susie, people teasing her like that – though it's OK me doing it cos I'm her brother. Hate anyone bullying anyone else as there's enough meanness in the world, what with Israel and Palestine and all that, without making it happen in school as well.

Friday 7th June Bog paper's back where it should be and the sniffing rate has dropped drastically. Susie's a different person – back to her usual argumentative self. Time for some more teasing, I reckon. Think I'M becoming allergic to my sisters. They're determined to reduce me to having streaming eyes too. Am going back to worrying about the more important things in life – like my zits, and how to get up close to Cills.

Saturday 8th June Thought I'd found a friend at last! A lovely thick envelope with my name on it arrived today – definitely not the usual reminder from the library about overdue books. Opened it with great expectations and found it was just the stuff for Susie on her hayfever. Here's some of it.

Hayfever: the facts

(1) There are 6,000,000 people who suffer from hayfever in England.

(2) There is no actual cure, though medicines help to prevent and treat it, and some people do grow out of it. This may not happen till you are 30 or 40.

This seems real ancient to me.

(3) There are skin tests where they inject you with a small extract of the pollens (in other allergies they use other substances like house dust or animal fur), usually on your arm. Some minutes later, if you are allergic, you get a small itchy swelling in the place where the prick was made. However, skin tests don't always work and they sometimes suggest you are allergic to a lot more things than you actually are.

What can be done to make it less uncomfortable?

The best way not to get hayfever is to avoid pollen; but this may not always be possible, and in many cases it is better to treat it than become a hermit. Ten handy tips which help are:

* Stay away from grassy areas.

* Take your holidays by the sea.

* Keep your house windows closed when your neighbours mow the grass.

* Remember there is more pollen about on hot days.

* Wear dark glasses out of doors.

* Avoid taking walks in the evening.

* Avoid trips in the countryside in June and July.

* Keep the car windows closed when in the car.

* Check the pollen forecast.

* Ask your doctor for advice and be sure to take the medicine prescribed. Antihistamines are the most common ones, but they can make you feel a bit sleepy.

Brilliant stuff! Might use this info to earn some extra cash by offering my services to the local radio station.

10

My **First Fag** Nearly Kills Me

Wednesday 12th June Feeling hard done by as all my mates have gone on a school field trip to Cornwall. Only 20 places and PP wasn't given one of them. We're having to WORK while they're having a good time, and we're being taught by really crap teachers while all the OK ones are off enjoying themselves on the trip. There's nothing on telly except *Neighbours*, and all the local films that I haven't seen are PG and not even worth considering.

After school, didn't particularly want to go home as Susie had gone to stay with her friend Kate again, and Mum and Dad were going to be away till late on Dad's work outing. Hope it'll make them nicer to one another, as they've been having more rows.

Was slowly drifting home, with nothing much to do, when I saw smoke signals going up from the Rec. Couldn't read the signals so went to investigate (this was me in my private detective role). Turned out it was some of my classmates trying to kill themselves with fags. Before I could open my mouth, they shouted, 'Here comes "Know all" Pete' and '"I know what's good for you" Pete' and '"You're killing yourselves" Pete'.

Cornered me, puffing smoke in my face and yelling, 'Yeh, yeh, we know, we know – don't cack yer pants, Pete.'

Gotta be crass and stupid that they still smoke, when it's gobsmackingly obvious from everything we've been told that :

>> it kills you – actively; and all those around you – passively

>> by the time we grow up, smoking will kill 7 million of us around the world each year

>> if we have four friends who smoke, at least two will die from it

>> in the UK, smoking kills nearly as many as a load of passengers on a Boeing 747, EVERY DAY

>> every cigarette knocks 5 minutes off our lives

>> it damages babies inside the womb

>> kissing a smoker is like kissing an ashtray.

What a load of tossers.

They were perfectly happy to yabber on about WHY they smoked, though. Rachel, who is in a wheelchair cos of having something called 'cerebral palsy', said that she started when she was 13. Her older sister's boyfriend was a heavy smoker. One night when their parents were out, he and her sister went to the back door (their mum wouldn't allow the smell inside the house) and began to smoke. *EastEnders* had finished, so Rachel went outside too. Her sister said jokingly, 'Would ya like to try a fag?' and she said OK, because she didn't want to look stupid in front of the boyfriend. Made her feel dizzy and hurt the back of her throat, but she carried on to impress her sister and the boyfriend. Now she gets her fags from the corner shop, or bums them off friends.

Dave got his fags from lots of different shops, and though he was only 14, he never had any trouble buying them. He enjoyed smoking cos he thought it made him look big and hard, and said that if someone wanted to smoke, it was up to them and nothing to do with anyone else. He started smoking when he and his cousin bought some fags and tried them down by the river. He didn't like them much, and at first only smoked at parties and when clubbing. Later he had lots of arguments with his mum and used to get very upset, but found that a fag 'sort of helped'. Funny thing is he hates girls smoking, as he thought it made them look common. Once at school he nearly got caught, so he stuffed the fag into his pocket and burnt himself. What a jerk.

Of course Monica had to butt in here cos she didn't see why girls smoking was any different from boys doing it. She thought it made HER look big and hard too, and kept her thin and made her sexier, which mattered to her more than dying a bit sooner (reckon that's stupid cos I know loads of thin people who don't smoke and anyhow, according to Sam's dad, it's not so much the dying early, but the falling to pieces, bit by bit, all the time that you're smoking that really matters). Monica didn't think there was any point in her giving up, as her sister smoked and her health was damaged cos she was breathing in her smoke anyhow. She didn't seem to care what happened in 20 years' time, as she reckoned we'd probably all be dead from toxic waste and fumes and things, now that America didn't care about the environment at all and were the worst polluters in the world.

Some kid that I had never talked to before said that he smoked at school every day and never got caught. He and his friends kept their lighted cigarettes in their desks and lifted up the top when they wanted a drag. Didn't think that the teachers cared much, as most of them smoked too, and you could smell Mr Rogers's fag-laden breath from half a mile away. But this kid wished he didn't smoke cos it was crippling with all the money he was spending on it – but he couldn't stop cos he was addicted to tobacco.

In the end they all insisted on me just trying, so I knew what I was missing. Made out there was something wrong with me if I didn't smoke – or was it that I was too soft to try? Actually I thought it would be bigger and harder of me NOT to try, but I'm just a 7-stone weakling when forced. Didn't feel too bad at first, though it made me want to cough. In my heavy detective role I took 2 or 3 more really deep drags – and the top of my head began to fall off. Started to cough worse, spluttering and spitting all over my mates and getting pins and needles feelings in my hands. Eyes began watering and I nearly passed out. When I began to look as if I was about to throw up, my classmates, who had been killing themselves laughing, all edged away at speed.

Staggered on home with a nasty song going through my mind, over and over again – 'The smoker is a silly tit, the fags just make you stink like shit'. Stopped at local newspaper shop to buy 5 packets of polos and some chewing gum to cover up the smell. Through my green sick haze all I could see were packets and packets of fags on the shelves and endless fag adverts. When I came out, staring me in the face across the road was a picture, 20 feet high, advertising more fags with tiny letters at the bottom saying 'DANGER – SMOKING CAN KILL'. It was only 25 yards from the local primary school entrance. Really sad – having it so close, where little kids can see it – must be against the law?

What a lot of arseholes – politicians letting cigarette companies have adverts all over the place knowing that thousands and thousands of people get killed by fags every year. Bloody lot of hypocrites, I reckon.

Got home, cleaned my teeth, ate a packet of polos, and held my breath when Mum kissed me goodnight – but she still gave me a look which said 'I know what you've been up to, Pete Payne' .

Thursday 13th June Came top in the maths test. Had two Mars Bars and a Crunchy to celebrate. Worried about a pain in my groin. Think it must be appendicitis, but according to the medical dictionary I should have a temperature and be throwing up, so can't be that.

Saturday 15th June Spent morning reading Sam's bike magazines. He still dreams of winning the Tour de France. Pain in my groin's gone. Funny how my body can have a pain one moment and then make it go without me knowing a thing about why I had it.

Thoughts interrupted by a scream from Susie, who'd been searching for sellotape for Mum's birthday card. She'd found some cigs in a tin Dad keeps odds and ends in on the top shelf in the kitchen. A month ago he'd promised he'd given up and was chewing this Nicorette gum stuff instead (though I guessed he hadn't stopped completely from the stink of fags in the garage). Susie and I decided this meant war. Down at the local toy shop bought a packet of cigarette bangers. Stuffed a couple into the end of his remaining three fags. The fag packet actually had written on it 'Protect Children – Don't Make Them Breathe Your Smoke'.

Susie and I kept looking at one another all afternoon and giggling. Mum and Dad knew something was up, but didn't tell them anything. Just before supper Dad disappeared upstairs to the loo. A minute later the loo exploded, followed by Dad shouting a four-letter word, VERY, VERY loud. It was the one that he keeps telling US never ever to use. Susie and I collapsed laughing and Mum gave us her LOOK. After 5 minutes dead silence Dad appeared, saying nothing but sucking a mint. I'm not half bad now at recognizing the smell of polo mints and cigarette smoke mixed, though Dad's smell seemed to have some gunpowder in it as well.

Supper was straaaaaiiiiinnnnned. Susie just couldn't resist repeating, all innocent like, something I'd told her. 'Dad, did you know that it was Sir Walter Raleigh who first brought tobacco to England in the 16th century, and that doctors used to think it was good for all sorts of things like gout, and head lice, and ulcers? But now the National Health Service is having to spend £1.6 billion each year looking after people with illnesses that are due to them smoking. Every year in the UK smoking kills 10 times more people than road traffic accidents, falls, murder, suicide and HIV infection all put together. And Dad, by the way, you know it makes you impotent. Are you sure you feel all right, Dad?' So angelic, my little sister.

Mum didn't suss, but Dad choked on his cream topping and looked like a naughty boy. In the end he had to laugh. 'Yup, smoking's a filthy habit and I hope you never try it. In fact, I'll give you £200 each if you haven't smoked by the time you're 21.'

I said that wasn't much compared with the £40,000 HIS smoking habit would cost him over a lifetime, and he didn't need to bribe US to stop US from smoking. I'm a right little hypocrite when I want to be. Ever since

Sam's dad had bribed HIM, I'd been looking for a way to get Dad to bribe me.

There was no stopping preacher Dad now. 'You've all the facts and it's got to be the stupidest thing to do. The worst thing is that once you've started like me, it's difficult to stop because it's so addictive.' Oh hell, it began to sound like another school lecture, until Susie burst into tears saying, 'You mustn't die, Dad. You still splutter and cough in the mornings, and when you smoke, we have to breathe in your fumes'.

Mum told us to stop nagging, or Dad would need another fag to calm his nerves. So told my latest cigarette joke to lighten things up:

Q. Why does a man have a dog with no legs called 'Cigarette'?

A. Because every night he takes him out for a drag.

Dead silence. It was lucky that it was my night for the washing-up.

Sunday 16th June Raining and nothing to do.

Monday 17th June Raining and school and too much to do.

Tuesday 18th June Dad's now got a right anti-smoking fixation. Maybe it's cos I cut a photo of a cancerous lung out of a magazine and left it in his lunch box. Discovered it torn up in the bin. Reckon he must feel real worried that his smoking will start us off. Sat us down after tea and read us this newspaper article about how one in three grown-ups who smoke regularly started before 9, and that children under the age of 16 smoke 1,154,000,000 cigarettes a year and spend over 2 million pounds on them each week, and that by year 10 at school one in four children smokes.

Asked Dad why he smoked, and he said it was because being addicted to nicotine was as difficult to kick as being addicted to heroin. He found he couldn't concentrate so well if he didn't smoke, and he liked the feel of a fag in his mouth, and the whole routine of lighting up. He was getting help to give up the addiction using nicotine patches, and might try sprays, or gum, or some new pills, but it was still real, real hard giving up. Dad reckons that it was more the fault of the tobacco companies, who knew all about how fags kill people but still didn't stop selling as many cigs as they could. He hopes that the tobacco companies get screwed by all those people with lung cancer suing them. The tobacco companies spend £100,000,000 a year in advertising telling us why we should smoke, and the government only spends about the same over 3 years telling us why we shouldn't – while collecting all that lovely tax earned from cigarette sales at the same time. Apparently the government makes 8 billion pounds every year from cigarettes taxes. No wonder they're not keen on banning cigarette advertising!

Thursday 20th June Dad's fixation is catching and I finally confessed to Susie that I'd tried one, and was totally convinced I might be hooked on fags for life. Susie said that I was mad (nothing new there). She had tried a fag at a party 2 years ago, and had hated it so much she had never tried again – and she reckoned fags were just another drug and should be made illegal. Both of us agreed it would be sad to miss the £200 Dad was offering, though. Went to find him – to take up his offer.

Friday 21st June Sally's not getting HER £200. She's put her jeans through the wash with a packet of fags in them. Whole wash got nicotine-stained and the machine's got blocked tubes. Mum's already furious with her cos instead of revising for her exams, she's been spending all her time rehearsing the school play and drinking down the pub – when she's not out clubbing.

11 **Pains,** Sprains and Wheezes

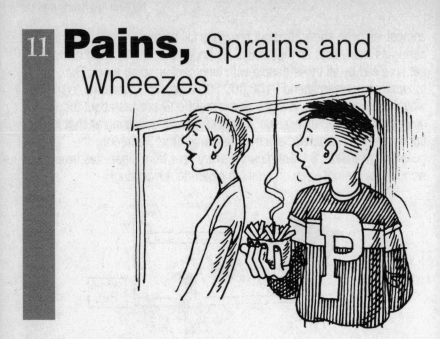

Tuesday 16th July Three more days to the summer hols. Can't wait. Went to McDonalds for chips on the way home today, and met Cills going in. Embarrassing as half the school were there, and it looked as if we were together. She's still obsessed with Randy Joe, mad cow disease, foot and mouth and everything, so wouldn't have a Big Mac.

Though I've fancied Cills for ages, don't reckon she knows how much. We're real good friends just now, but still don't know if I dare ask her out. Might say 'No' again. I've got to get sorted, as I can't go on fancying her and leave it at that. Suppose the easiest thing would be if you got to know someone really well first before asking them out. Hope this happens to me sometime cos at the moment I feel just hopeless about it all. Maybe I could do something like sending her a love heart by text message? Hope Randy Joe doesn't find out, though.

Wednesday 17th July Two days to summer hols. It's Sally's last term at school, and everyone's gone to watch her as Juliet in *Romeo and Juliet* this evening. Didn't go myself cos I've sat through it already, and anyhow

I know enough about family feuds, don't I? Perhaps I could learn a bit from R and J about what to say to Cills, though – something romantic without me feeling a total nerd.

Lounged around at home for the evening getting bored, so finally found myself in Susie's room. She'd forgotten to lock her diary so couldn't resist another peek. Can hardly read her handwriting. They ought to teach her that proper at school. Here we go…

Wednesday 3ʳᵈ July

Mum's cross because I haven't touched my flute for 3 days. Said it wasn't worth me having lessons if I didn't practise. What do grown-ups have to practise? It's not fair.

Thursday 4ᵗʰ July

'Came on' today. Second one ever. I'm glad I've started, but it's a bother – especially hiding the fact from Pete, who would tease me. Emailed Kate about it.

Blimey, must have missed that one…don't know how cos I snoop regular enough.

Favourite supper this evening – macaroni cheese and ice-cream. Perhaps I'll become a vegetarian and stop eating poor furry animals. No more little lambs with foot and mouth (wonder why humans don't get it?), but I know I won't be able to resist roast chicken, especially the way Mum cooks it. Told Pete I was going to be a vegetarian. He asked how I knew vegetables didn't feel just as much pain as animals. I couldn't answer, but I can't give up eating altogether or I'll get anorexic like Jane at school.

Got soaked running round the block with Kate, practising the 400 metres. I haven't been practising enough, so I think I'll probably come last. Only a week to go.

Saturday 8ᵗʰ July

I'm going to have a real moan. Pete's in a bad mood and taking it out on me. It's horrid being the youngest. My brother and sister always tease me, and when I react, they do it even more. They don't seem to mind how I feel, but when I tease them, they get angry and shout at me. They're sooooooo bossy. They think they can just tell me what to do and say. They all humiliate me in front of my friends, and it isn't fair, especially when Mum and Dad do it as well.

I'm so fed up with wearing grim, hand-me-down, cast-offs from Sally and Pete, especially as I think I'm getting fat. Last time I managed to get Mum to buy me something new, Sally teased me about trying to be 'cool'. Bet she was just the same when she was my age. And Sally and Pete are always trying to point out all the advantages I have – like staying up later than they did 'when they were my age', and getting more pocket money than they did 'when they were my age', and being allowed the last lick of the cake bowl, and on, and on.

Sunday 9ᵗʰ July

Went running. Tried to get Pete to come, but he stayed in bed and said he'd time me while I was gone. Bouncing Sally came instead. At least I'm faster than her. Pete was asleep when I got back. Lazy slob.

Bovril's going to the vet. No more kittens for her. Sally's got a new boyfriend, called Steve.

Wednesday 10ᵗʰ July

Dear diary,

All my practice wasted! I'm sitting here with my ankle wrapped in an 'elastic' bandage. Feels like a boa constrictor wrapped around a tree trunk.

Kate, Rani and me decided, as it was the last practice before Sports Day, we'd do a whole lot of false starts, which was fine until Miss 'Big Bum' Court got fed up. When we finally got started, we agreed that we'd all join hands and come in last together to show her. Rani reckons she's really faster than us, so just before crossing the finishing line, she let go and ran over the line first. I tripped over my other foot, fell flat on my face, and twisted my ankle. What really annoys me is that, in spite of my hayfever, I'm actually faster than Rani, but with a twisted ankle I won't get a chance to show her: I could kill her.

After the fall, I kept collapsing with pain, as my ankle wouldn't stay straight, and I cried because I thought it was broken. So I took my shoe and sock off and gently felt around like they said in the First Aid course. Sure it wasn't actually broken, so I limped over to Miss Court.

She got Mr Jones to carry me to the sick room, with the boys saying things like, 'What will your boyfriend say?' and 'teacher's pet' and 'I hope you don't herniate yourself, Mr Jones'. Then Miss Court appeared with a packet of frozen peas from the kitchens, muttering 'RICE PAD, RICE PAD, RICE PAD'. Thought she'd flipped till she explained that that is how she remembers what to do with bruises and sprains, and how to check that bones aren't broken. 'RICE' is for treating sprains: Rest, Ice, Compression, Elevation. 'PAD' is for checking for broken bones: Pain, Abnormal mobility, Deformity.

Had a quick check myself with PAD. There was lots of pain, but luckily not when Miss Court just pulled or pushed my foot, only when she twisted it. I could move it OK myself (with pain), and there didn't seem to be any worse deformity than what Pete says I have anyway. They bandaged my ankle up with an elastic bandage (compression — and how!), told me to keep the frozen peas on it when I got home (ice), and to put my leg on a chair or something when sitting (elevation). My shoe had suddenly grown very small because of the bandage and swelling, so they found a slipper from lost property. When it was time to go home, I was walking, or rather limping, but suddenly my ankle gave way again so a teacher got Kate to help me.

Got home feeling tired and depressed. Mum was nice, treating me as if I was a baby again, and gave me my supper on the settee. Later went to bed, but couldn't sleep. Was in so much pain I could've screamed. I tried to find a comfortable way to lie, and finally Mum came in and gave me some paracetamol. After a while I must have fallen asleep, and when I woke up it was morning.

I was 10 minutes late getting up, so jumped out of bed, forgetting I had a bad foot, and screamed because it hurt so much. Mum took me to the doctor, who turned out to be a real sports injuries pro. He said it was just bruised, not to walk on it for a day, and then gradually start walking on it with the bandage on, though it would probably go on hurting for a week or two but paracetamol would help the pain.

Gave me a lecture on how 80% of these injuries could be avoided if only everyone prepared properly for training and competition by being fit for their sports, by being careful about warming up and warming down before and afterwards, and by making sure they used the right equipment and techniques. Asked Mum about getting me new trainers.

Friday 12th July

Sports Day at school. The field was so wet, thought it might be postponed and then I could've run after all. During the morning I tried to teach Kate tactics to beat Rani, as we were still cross with her for causing my accident. We thought we might demand a drugs test on Rani. She looks as if she's on steroids, anyhow. It's sad anyone having to use drugs to win, especially famous people.

Sports Day wasn't put back, and had to sit on the wet grass and watch and freeze. Felt sorry for lovely Sam, as he had an attack of asthma during his run and came in last. While I was watching, I kept Rachel company. She goes everywhere in a wheelchair. She can't use her legs because of something called cerebral palsy that she's had from birth. I'd never talked to her before, but she's really nice. Must be awful for her, never being able to run. She wants to go in for a wheelchair marathon when she's old enough.

When the 400 metres was called, I felt this kind of knot in my tummy for Kate. Funny how nervous I can get for someone else. They were really close at the finish, but Rani won. Had to pretend to be pleased for her, even though my best time had been 3 seconds faster. As we were sitting there making friendship bracelets, Rachel and me were a captive audience. Everybody came to sympathize and then ended up telling us about their own problems.

John said that when he was playing football another player had done a sliding tackle. He fell in a funny way and twisted his ankle, which swelled up like a balloon. He had gone to the hospital where they X-rayed it and said there was nothing wrong. A couple of weeks later he had gone to stamp on a friend's foot, missed and twisted his ankle again.

Eddie Marley had been knocked out playing goalie. The ball was kicked towards him, he dived for it, and the full force of a defender's boot hit his head. He didn't know how long he was out, *but people told him it was half a minute. He remembered getting up with the help of his coach, but he was staggering all over the place. Although he felt quite clear-headed at half-time, at the end of the game he couldn't remember what had happened or what the score was. He got home and was sick and sleepy and had to go to hospital.*

Football certainly seems dangerous because then Timmy said that when he'd played in goal someone had kicked his arm instead of the ball, and then stood on it. He was taken off to

hospital with it broken. Meant he couldn't do any work, as it was his right arm, but he couldn't play football either!

Jan had bruised her bum and broken her collar bone when SHE went over a jump and her horse didn't. She was taken to the medical tent, where they put a funny bandage round her shoulders, but her own doctor had taken it off. He said that although normally one had to stop broken bones from moving for them to mend (like when Pete broke his arm and had a plaster), the collar bone would heal up OK by itself.

I was saved from any more of these horror stories by kind Mum, who came to take me home. Wish my ankle would get better.

I bet dick-head Dave didn't tell her about the time he twisted his bollocks doing a one-handed hopping handstand, and had to have THEM put into plaster. I'd read enough.

Friday 19th July Last day of school – yippeee. No one did any work. Don't know why we bother to go in.

Sam's not coming with us to France these hols. His whole family is going to Italy on a 'package' – Sam's dad booked it over the internet, so Sam reckons they may never get there. Sam's usually first or second in cross-country, while Randy Joe and me hide in the pack. But on Sports Day last week he was last in the 100 metres and collapsed, wheezing horribly, till someone gave him his inhaler to puff. Uses it quite often, especially before he runs. Sam reckons his asthma is getting worse cos of the increased pollution around…reckons he'll also sue America for not signing the Kyoto agreement…Sam's so brill at everything and knows everything – I really hate him sometimes. Showed him the stuff about asthma that came with the leaflet on hayfever from the radio station in case there was something he didn't know…

It said asthma is a disease of the lungs in which the muscles round the air passages get all tight. The air passages, or 'bronchioles', as the leaflet called them, get narrowed, and stop the easy flow of air into, and especially out of, the air sacs where the oxygen in the air normally crosses into the blood inside the lungs. People with asthma not only get wheezy, but feel as if they are suffocating as well, which is very frightening. Under the section 'WHAT CAUSES ATTACKS' it said:

Asthma is not infectious. It's just that the air passages in the lungs of asthmatic children are very sensitive and their narrowing can be set off by many different things: changes in the weather, particularly cold weather or strong winds; pollution; emotional strains such as excitement, or prolonged laughing; infections (colds which go to the chest); exercise (Sam's main problem) and allergy. Allergy is a special form of sensitivity in which substances that don't affect most people start attacks in those with asthma. Common things that people are allergic to include house dust, grass pollen, and fur and skin flakes from animals.

A lot of the allergy stuff sounded just like hayfever, without the runny eyes. I'm still waiting to see what I'm allergic to (not counting my Mum saying I'm allergic to hard work). The leaflet went on:

Treatment of Asthma

Present-day treatment does not cure asthma, but it usually enables children with quite severe asthma to lead a normal life. To do this they may need to take medicines during school hours. These medicines are of two different types:

(1) Treatment which the child takes when the wheezing has started. This is usually in the form of a spray called Salbutamol (Ventolin) to be breathed into the lungs. It gives immediate relief by relaxing the lung muscles and opening up the narrowed air passages.

(2) Treatment which decreases the sensitivity of the lungs to what normally sets off an attack, and so prevents the narrowing of the air passages and the resulting wheezing. This treatment may also be a medicine to be breathed in, called Beclomethasone (Becotide), also called the preventer.

If these medicines are not taken regularly and properly, severe asthma may develop.

This bit of the leaflet reminded me of the time Sam was had up in front of the head for using his inhaler, cos his arsehole of a teacher thought he was taking illegal drugs!

Monday 22nd July Have to seek Dad's advice on sex after all. Mr Rogers has set us homework on 'Contraception' and 'Sexually Transmitted Diseases' – disgusting – with 7 sheets of questions to be answered by next term. What a way to spend the holidays – finding out about sex! Could be fun, though, if I can get some hands-on experience!

12

Sick, Sick, Sick

or the Summer Holidays

Friday 26th July Asked Mum whether Gran could be euthanased now she's so old, so I don't have to share a tent with her in France. I do love her, though. Mum was horrified that I even knew about euthanasia – but I reckon the world is becoming overcrowded with old people. Anyhow Gran's not coming camping with us after all. She's going to Bournemouth instead. Saved from sharing with Susie, too, as my friend Eddie is coming instead of Sam, and bringing his two-man tent.

Eddie's dead lucky getting two holidays and all – first one with us while his mum works, and then in Scotland with her. Hopes he'll go for a holiday in Jamaica with his Dad next year.

Saturday 27th July Not so sure I go for hols. Mum's ordered me to pack my own stuff. Dad's said 'One case only' as he isn't having any last-minute plastic bags under the seats or blocking his rear view in the car.

Did a great job – all my minidiscs, my heads, fishing tackle, penknife, medical dictionary, *Catcher in the Rye* and a few girlie boob mags, my zit creams, antiperspirant spray, athletes' foot powder, new trainers, and the first-aid book and kit Uncle Bob gave me last Christmas. Enough to equip a field hospital for a full-scale disaster. Contains: tube of Savlon, 20 swabs, 10 non-adherent Melonin dressings, 25 adhesive plasters, 3 bandages, 20 paracetamol, 10 magnesium trisilicate compound tablets for indigestion, Calamine cream, scissors and tweezers. Hope I get a chance to use them.

Didn't pack anything else cos there wasn't room. Unfortunately Mum decided to check. She's impossible. Made me take most of my gear out and put some clothes in instead. So stuffed the books and medicines into a plastic bag, and hid them under the car seat.

Long argument between Mum and Dad about why she needed to take her whole wardrobe, plus the kitchen sink. Had to go back three times – first for Mum's bikini top, which was still on the washing line, then for my swimming trunks, and finally for Susie's sleeping bag. Then we had to stop in a lay-by near Maidstone. Eddie had suddenly gone silent and puked over Susie and the sleeping bags. Heard Dad mutter that we'd make Dover in 3 months if we were lucky.

While Mum mopped up, I looked up 'motion sickness' in my medical dictionary. No one knows exactly what causes it, but involves the middle part of the ear, which is to do with balance, and also the eyes. Deaf mutes don't get it, and Eddie was in good company – Julius Caesar, Lord Nelson, Charles Darwin and Lawrence of Arabia were all travel pukers. Wouldn't want to be the next person to stop at that lay-by.

Was sent into the chemist at Dover for travel-sick pills instead of Susie, who's still pretending her ankle's wobbly. It's fine when she wants it to be. Packet said that the pills must be taken well in advance of travelling, and that they: *'May cause drowsiness. If affected, do not drive or operate machinery. Avoid alcoholic drink.'*

Waves coming over the harbour walls persuaded Mum and Susie to try the travel-sick pills as well as Eddie. Dad doesn't get sea-sick, and I just KNEW it wouldn't happen to me. I may be a hypochondriac but I'm not a weakling. Anyway, the instructions that came with the pills also gave hints how real men like me can avoid getting travel sick:

At sea

When possible, stay on deck and look at the horizon. Keep away from diesel and galley smells. Avoid rich and fatty foods. If below decks, lie face down with eyes closed.

On the road

If possible, look forward into the distance. Try to ensure children can see out of windows. Avoid reading while in motion. Travel by daylight if possible. Ensure fresh air and no fumes. Avoid rich and fatty foods.

On the boat downed chips, bacon, eggs and sausages, as did Eddie and Susie. Wasted all of mine throwing up and left it feeding the seagulls in the Channel. Eddie and Susie sneaked off and won the jackpot on the fruit machines. Will have to take the sea-sick pills next time, or even better get Dad to put the car on the train through the Tunnel.

Sunday 28th July This is being written wearing a sad, soggy, embarrassing T-shirt with 'SHIT HAPPENS' on it – in a soggy sleeping bag, in a soggy tent, in a French mud patch called a camping site, somewhere in Brittany. Might as well be in our back garden. Desperate for a pee. Don't know where to go. It's already daylight, so can't go outside and let it rip. Sooooo hungry after the sea pukes. Eddie's still asleep, knackered after talking most of the night about his parents and what it was like when they got divorced.

Said it was terrible at first – all that shouting and arguing. He'd wondered whether it was something he'd done wrong, but it obviously wasn't. Then he'd worried that if they didn't love one another, perhaps they didn't love him either. When his dad finally left and went back to Jamaica, Eddie had begun wetting his bed every night, but he didn't anymore (was I glad to hear that!). Said that, although separated parents weren't what he would choose to have, it was better than having parents who lived together but didn't speak to each other, or had horrendous arguments all the time.

Luckily, Eddie's divorced parents still do talk to one another and are actually quite friendly. A bad thing was he didn't see enough of his dad, who's in Jamaica, but he also worried about his mum being lonely when he was away with his dad.

He reckoned the great thing was still living in the same house as he was brought up in, so that he still had all the other things that he was used to, since as far back as he could remember. But his dad and his new partner had a baby boy who he hoped to see next year.

If this had been the only thing I'd heard about parents getting divorced, think I'd have had a word with my own, but it seems to have been worse for some of my other friends. God, I'm desperate. I'll burst if I don't find a pissary somewhere.

Saturday 3rd August Too depressed to write for a week. Rain, rain, rain, rain, rain. Reckon I've seen the inside of more churches than the Pope. All dead boring. How it's 'good for you' I don't know. I'm not even holy, just an existential agnostic, devoted to the dot com economy, the money market – and my tackle.

Talking of tackle, life hasn't been all good for Susie either. In the last cathedral she was lighting up a candle to the Patron Saint of Animals, or someone, and turned round to find an old man with his mackintosh open, flashing his dick. Said her first reaction was 'ugh', not at what he was doing but at the actual thing itself cos it looked so puny and wrinkled. Was also surprised and shocked (not being the sort of thing one normally expects in a cathedral), but then thought 'be smart, don't scream or cry or run away. That's what pervs want you to do. Just be cool and leave'.

So she walked away. The guy must've been real miffed.

Sunday 4th August Poor Susie. Flashed at yesterday, pukes and runs today. Wonder if it's all psychological? She said it was bad enough getting the runs at the best of times, but on a holiday campsite with the lavs made of concrete and smelling of stale pee! Wants to go home. Wish she would, she's becoming a real pain.

Dad said her shits were from eating too many peaches. Eddie said it was the water. I think it was all in her mind. But Mum said the doctor told her that people often get upset tummies abroad because they come into contact with lots of new tummy bugs. Said it wasn't usually serious, only lasted a couple of days, and normally got better without having to spend money on medicines. Instead, Susie had to stop eating and drink lots of clear fluids, like water or weak fruit juices, a little at a time so that she didn't puke up again.

My medical dictionary was full of different names for the shits in different parts of the world: Hong Kong Dog, Delhi Belly, Aztec Two-step, Rangoon Runs. Don't think Susie's was much like any of these. More like 'Silly Susie's Sloppy French Shits'. Hope it's cholera.

Monday 5th August No sleep. Susie tripped over our tent pegs all last night. Wonder if she made it to the lavs or if I'll be stepping in her crap when I need to go? She gave us all the messy details this morning over coffee and croissants.

Having the runs meant she worried whether she'd do it in her knickers before she got to the toilets, or before she'd finished puking. Said she had a really heavy feeling in her arms and legs, dead annoying because she couldn't be bothered to think or do anything. The worst thing, though, was actually being sick and not knowing whether the shits would come out at the same time. She said her bum was sore and itched, so Mum gave her my Savlon cream to put on. Suppose I need it? What then?

SUNNY DAY! At last a chance to get my HE-MAN tan. Perhaps my acne will improve too. Might even disappear altogether! Mutiny at Dad's suggestion of going to local nudy beach. Not taking ALL my clothes off. Susie, who has almost NOTHING to show anyhow, refuses to go topless. Wish Mum would refuse as well. She might have a bit of consideration for Eddie. Dead embarrassing

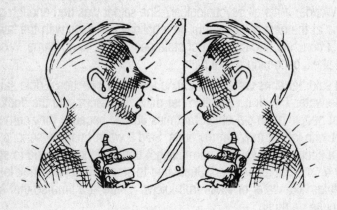

Tuesday 6th August Arrgggh – the agony. Feels like a thousand needles are being shoved about under my skin. Can't bear the touch of anything. Even if Cills put her naked body next to mine, I'd scream for her to go away. Promise I would. None of me's brown, just bright red like an over-cooked tomato. Am lying in my tent wearing Calamine cream and nothing else. Everyone else is in the sun. Clever me. Didn't listen to Mum, did I, when she said put some lotion on and take it easy in the sun.

Spent whole day displaying my muscles, with only my swimming trunks on (at least THAT bit of me is spared – I'm even gladder we refused to go to the nudist beach). Wasn't till evening my skin really caught fire. Took some paracetamol for the pain. Smart-arse Susie read out the French notice on the camp board. It said:

ATTENTION!
IL EST TRÈS DANGEREUX DE RESTER AU SOLEIL...

She waited till Eddie was around to impress him with her translation: 'Look out, it is very dangerous to lie around in the sun for long periods of time. Only expose your skin to the sun for short periods, and particularly avoid the middle of the day when the sun is strongest. Use appropriate sun-tan lotions (high block), especially if you have fair and sensitive skin. Wear a hat to protect your head from direct sunlight. Too much sun may lead to skin cancer.' Dunno where she learnt all that French from, maybe it's that Jean guy she's been hanging around with here. Reckon Eddie's not going to have this problem.

Wednesday 7th August WORSE...WORSER... weepy blisters everywhere and bits of skin peeling off. Mum says it's only my outer layer! My dictionary says when we get burnt, all the cells in this layer die and are removed by what's called 'serous' fluid. Luckily if the burns are not too deep, the body just grows a new layer of skin to take its place. I'm busy drinking lots of coke to make up for all the wet coming off me (including the sweat!), and eating tons of French bread, butter and paté, with fruit and chocolate and sloppy cheeses, to help my poor old body remake itself.

Book says that getting brown happens when cells in the skin called 'melanocytes' start making a pigment called 'melanin', which filters the sunlight and stops it from being able to burn the skin. Hope there'll be a chance for my melanocytes to get going before the next downpour.

Susie's getting her own back for my lack of sympathy over her 'French Shits' – poking her mug into the tent, not asking me how I am, just staring and bursting out laughing, and then disappearing off with Eddie.

Thursday 8th August More late-night discussion, with bugs smashing around the tent. Susie and Eddie on about divorce again. Susie was horrified when Eddie said that nowadays more than one in three marriages ends in divorce, and that half the children of these broken marriages lose contact with one of their parents. Eddie reckoned that a common effect of divorce on children was they started to do much worse at school, which is what happened to him. Wonder if that's what's happened to the Royals? – though maybe they didn't have any brains to start with.

Susie said her friend Pam's parents were divorced and Pam hardly saw her dad, but she felt she had grown away from him completely, and although he was her biological father, she didn't actually like him much. She knew he wanted to see her more, but it was a 'duty' for her, and a real drag having to leave her friends and go somewhere where she didn't know anybody. What's more, everyone expected her to be good friends with her stepsister, who got on her nerves 90% of the time.

Wasn't Eddie's experience, but it's obviously different for everybody. All his friends whose parents were having 'problems' or getting divorced came to him, cos they thought he would know what they were going through – the arguments, the door-slamming, the accusations, the tears, the feeling it was all their fault, the long silences, the guilt, the resentment.

Blisters better. Even a tinge of brown, but still very scared about the sun. Looking forward to going home. Susie said she wished I'd go now.

Friday 9th August Susie and Eddie are covered with plague. Probably mosquito bites. Hope they get malaria. Offered my Savlon (what's not been used up on Susie's bum) and Calamine in return for an ice-cream bought from their fruit-machine winnings. Dad said no chance of malaria cos French-type mosquitoes don't carry it. Itching and red bumps (Mum's got them too) are the body reacting to the bugs' saliva, which they inject when they bite. Yuck!

Saturday 10th August Made it home, loaded with cheap fags, wine and beer which Dad says are 'for someone at work'! Postcard from Cills saying she's brown all over. Forget what I said about rejecting her naked body.

Bovril's fleas leapt up to greet us. Popped her into a string bag and sprayed her all over with de-fleaing stuff – another enemy for life. Mobile working again – message from Sam: 'Welcum back – CU L8R 2day'. Must give him a bell.

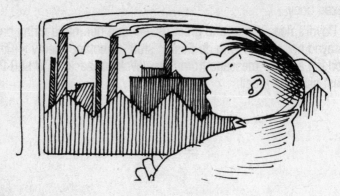

13

Fears about the **Future**

Tuesday 3rd September Cills is really brown – but is it all over?
Didn't dare ask her. Maybe I'll text-message the question…noooooo.
DETERMINED to be her boyfriend, though.

Wednesday 4th September Only back at school a day and they're
already going on about GCSEs and assessments. Seems nothing else is
going to matter from now on. Been given a timetable for the term, which
looks horrific, and a note to say that our exercise books mustn't have any
graffiti on them – it's like they're exam police or something. Maybe they
think that otherwise computer games will rule over us. Mum and Dad
have to sign a homework diary and say what THEY think about my work.

Monday 9th September Yesterday was Sam's birthday treat. He's 15.
Too wiped out to write last night after 360 miles in his dad's Audi TT and
3 hours at a rough amusement park. Sam, Eddie and myself. Was more
fun than usual, as took car-sick pills for the journey and was able to

stand up to Sam's dad's driving (almost as bad as Mum's). Even managed the Nemesis, Multiversion Roller Coaster, where you end up sitting on your head as you go over the top completely hanging in suspension, all without a whiff of throwing up. Were long queues for everything, but took it in turns waiting while the others went off for hamburgers and pees.

On the motorway, passed over really depressing, endless rows of tiny dirty streets below. Sam's dad said that poverty was the worst health problem that the world had and the UK was no exception, with 90% of the population earning less than £30,000 a year. Been like that ever since Margaret Thatcher was in power, and even now the gap between rich and poor is getting bigger.

Unemployment is a major health problem as well. Doctors had found that unemployment not only caused feelings of helplessness and depression, and attempted suicide (apparently the risk was increased by nine times in the unemployed), but also physical problems like heart and lung diseases as well.

Felt real depressed at all this. Actually something I worry about a lot, especially now Sally's failed her exams, doesn't have a job, and doesn't know what to do. Must be awful not having a job you like, and worse if you're young and there looks as if there's no hope for the rest of your life. Nearly one million are unemployed, but there's talk of all this recession business now. Can sure understand someone without a job wanting to do themselves in. Government keeps talking about the 'feel-good factor', but I don't know where it is, especially if Dad loses his job. Maybe I'll have to get a job in another country now we're in Europe. Quite fancy France myself cos of the pretty filles there but will have to parlez le langue a bit better.

Sam's more worried about war, and what is going on in Israel and Palestine and Afghanistan and all the rest. He's really upset about all the money spent on guns and planes and stuff, when it could be used to feed starving people. Eddie reckoned that when there's a war, it should get rid of unemployment, either by killing us all or by us all having to fight in the army. He thinks the last world war looked really great from the TV series on 'The World at War'. Daft idea which made Sam's dad swerve across the road, nearly crashing into the back of a huge transporter lorry carrying imported Japanese cars. Just missed it, so no end to the worries about being unemployed.

Wednesday 18th September Got back all the work I'd done for Mr Rogers over the summer hols. Mine was best in the class, but all my friends wanted to know how come I knew so much about sexually transmitted diseases. OK, it was mainly from Dad – but didn't let on. They said was it going to France for my holidays? I said 'Yes', cos actually a bit was the hours lying in sunburnt agony in my tent, reading my medical dictionary. But left them imagining other things! Here's some of what I'd done…

You'd better learn this or there will be a lot of unwanted Paynes in the world!

Name Peter Payne

CONTRACEPTION

1. Before an egg can grow into a fully formed baby it must be

Fertilized ✓

2. How many eggs are released each month?

Two or three   *Usually one*

3. How many sperms are contained in an average ejaculation?

100,000,000 ✓

4. How many sperms are needed to fertilize one egg?

One ✓

5. How long can sperm live inside a woman's body?

About three days ✓

6. How can a woman get pregnant if a man does not reach a climax
(ejaculate)?   *Men leak sperm even before
they ejaculate*

She can't

7. What does contraception mean? Ways of stopping
getting pregnant when making love ✓

8. What are the chances of a girl getting pregnant if she has sexual
intercourse once without contraception 14 days before her next
period? Don't know. *1 in 3 chance — very risky!*

9. What is a condom? It's like a long rubber ✓
balloon you put on your penis before making love

10. Give another name for a condom: Rubber, Durex, Sheath,
Johnny, French letter, Japanese wrinkle ✓
?

93

11. How do condoms work? Stop the sperm getting spilt into the woman's vagina ✓

12. Are condoms reliable? Yes ✓

13. What are the advantages of condoms? Easy to use. Easy to keep around if you suddenly want to make love, cheap, easy to buy ✓ anywhere, everybody knows about them and they protect against sexually transmitted diseases, including Aids & cervical cancer.

14. What is an oral contraceptive? A hormone pill that women swallow ✓

15. How does the Pill work? Kills the egg No — not stop the ova from being released from the ovary. A few stop the fertilized egg from being implanted.

16. How reliable is the Pill? Most reliable method available at the moment ✓

17. What are the disadvantages of the Pill? Don't know It interferes with women's hormones. You have to see a doctor to get it. It also doesn't protect you against getting Aids & other STDs.

18. What is the contraceptive injection? This is a hormone which needs to be injected every 3 months.

19. How does the injection work? It stops the egg being released and thickens the mucus around the cervix (neck of womb), so the sperm can't get through. It's 99% effective but doesn't stop infections getting through ✓

20. What is the proper name for the withdrawal method? Coitus Interruptus ✓

21. Is the withdrawal method a reliable method of contraception?
It's OK   No - it's very unreliable - but better than nothing.

22. How does the rhythm or natural method work? By not having sex near the time when the egg is released ✓ (called ovulation)

23. Is the rhythm method very reliable? Yes.
No, it's not a safe method. Lots of people get pregnant this way because

24. What are the disadvantages of the rhythm method?
Don't know   it's very difficult to know when ovulation occurs, and people often want to make love when it's not a safe time.

25. What is an IUD? Intra-uterine device ✓

26. Is an IUD reliable? Yes ✓

27. How does an IUD work? Stops fertilized egg ✓ from becoming implanted in the womb

28. Are there any disadvantages in using an IUD? Yes - falls out all the time   Sometimes, but main problem is risk of infection in young women.

29. Give another word for a diaphragm: cap ✓

30. How is a diaphragm used? It's put into the vagina before making love and covers the ✓ cervix to stop the sperm reaching the ovum

31. Is the diaphragm method safe? Yes. Hope so. I think my mum uses it

32. What are the advantages of the diaphragm? *Don't know. Never tried it.* Safe., protects against some STDs., doesn't interfere with the woman's hormones.

33. Are there any disadvantages to using a diaphragm? *Don't know* Always have to remember to put it in before making love.

34. What is a spermicidal chemical? *Kills sperms dead.* ✓

35. How are spermicidal chemicals used? *Should be used with diaphragm and condoms.* ✓

36. Are spermicidal chemicals safe? *No, not on their own*

37. What is involved in sterilization? *The fallopian tubes in the woman or the spermatic ✓ cords in the man are cut and/or tied*

38. Is sterilization a reliable method of contraception? *Yes if the doctor does it right*

39. Are there any disadvantages to sterilization? *No. Yes — it's difficult to change your mind if you want to have babies later.*

DISEASES ASSOCIATED WITH SEX ✓

1. What does STD stand for? *Sexually transmitted disease*

2. Give the names of four STDs:

(a). *AIDS*

(b) *Chlamydia*

(c) *Penile and vaginal warts*

(d) *Gonorrhea*

3. **Can they be transmitted by**

(a) Lavatory seats *Probably* ~~no~~

(b) Kissing *No* ✓

(c) French kissing *Unlikely* ✓

(d) Vaginal intercourse *Yes* ✓

(e) Holding hands *No* ✓

(f) Anal intercourse *Yes* ✓

(g) Masturbation *No* ✓

4. **What causes the following sexually transmitted diseases?**

(a) Acquired Immune Deficiency Syndrome (Aids) *Rampant virus* ✓ HIV

(b) Chlamydia *Don't know* A kind of bacteria

(c) Syphilis *A micro thing* – called a spirochaete

(d) Non-specific urethritis (NSU) *A sort of bacteria* ✓

(e) Thrush *A kind of mushroom* a yeast

(f) Vaginal and penile warts *Virus* ✓

(g) Herpes *Herpes simplex virus* ✓ ✓

(h) Crabs *Lice that live in the pubic hair* Yes, but different from the head ones.

(i) Gonorrhoea *Don't know* a bacteria

97

5. **Aids**

How do you know you have it? You feel incredibly ill and weak – get lumps in your glands all over your body. but you can carry the virus and be infectious but not be ill yourself.

How can you treat it? You can't. You can't cure it but there are drugs which slow it down

How can you reduce the risk of getting it? Don't sleep.✓ around. Don't be a drug addict. Use condoms for sex. One partner only is safest.

What happens if you don't treat it? You die – but not everyone does. and, as you say above, there's no treatment.

6. **Gonorrhoea**

How do you know you have it? You get pus coming out of your penis✓ Women get a discharge from their vagina.

How can you treat it? With penicillin – discovered by Alexander Fleming – wonder if he had it?

7. **Thrush**

How do you know you have it? ~~You have little mushrooms and things~~ You get a red, itchy penis or vagina. It's not always a sexually transmitted disease.

How can you treat it? Go to a clinic✓ or to your GP – it's very easily treated with a cream.

How can you reduce the risk of getting it? Don't know. It's very common & usually not a problem.

What happens if you don't treat it? Don't know...... You just stay itching.

8. **Vaginal and penile warts**

How do you know you have them? You can see them.

How can you treat them? You can pick them off. No – there's a special paint you can get from your doctor.

How can you reduce the risk of getting them? Don't have sex with someone who has them. ✓

What happens if you don't treat them? Nothing much but nobody wants to know you ✓

9. **Herpes**

How do you know you have it? You get a coldsore of the penis or vagina ✓ Not a joking matter

How can you treat it? No treatment. (Joke – what's the difference between herpes and love? Answer – herpes is forever.)

How can you reduce the risk of getting it? Not sleeping with

What happens if you don't treat it? anyone who's got it Pops up now and then ✓

10. **Non-specific urethritis (NSU)**

How do you know you have it? ＊ It hurts when you pee ✓

How can you treat it? No sex or alcohol for 3 weeks – and take an antibiotic

How can you reduce the risk of getting it? Don't have sex with anyone who has it – and using Japanese wrinkles = condoms? If so, yes.

What happens if you don't treat it?

Goes on hurting and you pass it on.

got it, but can pass it on

99

11. Which of the following is correct about the virus which causes Aids?

(a) It is only a homosexual disease *Mostly* *Not true.* *Most cases in the world are caused by sex between men & women — although most cases in the UK are from sex between men & men.*

(b) Men and women can catch it *True* ✓

(c) There is no real danger from it *false* ✓

(d) More than 25,000 people in Britain have it *True. I hope I'm not one of them.* *So do I!*

(e) At the moment the disease is incurable *True*

(f) Drug addicts are at increased risk *True*

(g) Using condoms helps prevent getting it *True*

(h) Having sex with lots of people makes you more likely to get it
True

12. Crabs (or pubic lice)   *Girls get itchy in their pubic hair*

How do you know you have them? *You get itchy round your balls.*

How can you treat them? *Use a special lotion from the chemist (Durbac) or burn them with a lighter* — *no!! Would be very painful.*

How can you reduce the risk of getting them? *Don't sleep with anyone who has them.* ✓

What happens if you don't treat them? *You get more and more of them.* ✓

13. Chlamydia

How do you know you have it? *Don't know*

How can you treat it? *Don't know*

How can you reduce the risk of getting it? *Don't know*

What happens if you don't treat it? *Don't know*

14. **What should you do if you think you might have a sexually transmitted disease?** *Go to your doctor or to a special clinic for sexually transmitted diseases in a hospital* ✓

Very good, Pete, BUT

You need to know about chlamydia. It's now the commonest sexually transmitted infection in young people. It's caused by a very sneaky kind of bacteria — over half the people who have caught it don't know, as it doesn't produce any symptoms, but it can cause infertility and problems with getting pregnant when you want to. Sometimes it can cause pain on peeing or a penile or vaginal discharge, or bleeding after sex in women. The good news is it's easy to be tested for it & treated with antibiotics, which cure you & stop it being spread to others.

101

Thursday 19th September Totally depressed. Asked Cills to the cinema and she said 'No'. Curled up inside. Why does it hurt so, and makes me feel so hopeless?

Don't think my ego can take it. Sam got the nomination for class rep on the school council instead of me.

Friday 20th September Sticking in my monitoring form from previous week – praise from Mum at last, ego certainly needs it! This is what everyone said, including me!

MONITORING FORM

Homework and planning for week's work

Explain what will happen in diagram of energy changes and particles

Mystery plays

Who was most responsible for Eva's death?

Find out why castles declined

Write out arguments for and against private schools

Student's comments and targets

(records of achievements made this week, problems encountered, targets set for the future, items to remember, etc.)

Aim to work HARDER in some classes. Be seen to make an effort (don't chat!). Try harder in PE. Pleased with my knowledge about sex but not much progress with it.

Teacher's comments

Pete has done some good work this week, especially in maths. I'm concerned that he was late handing in his first English assignment. He tends to leave some homework until the last minute.

Parents' comments

We are very pleased with him. He seems to be making progress. We are particularly impressed with how much he knows about sex.

Wish mum had left that sex bit out – decided against tippexing it out, though.

14

Too Fat, Too Thin, Too Little, Too Large

Tuesday 24th September Susie's mad at me cos I opened one of her letters 'by mistake'. Like doing that – gives me a high. It was from someone who writes the agony page for *Teenage Weekly* – the next best thing to *Sugar*. Seems Susie must have written to this Agony Aunt character about being overweight. Can't really see why. It said:

Agony Column
Teenage Weekly
Wigmore Road
London WC1

Dear Susie

Thank you for your letter.

You say that you are overweight, and always have been, and having recently lost 2 kilos, you have put 1.5 kilos back. You insist that you are constantly trying to lose weight!

You also write that some of your family are unsympathetic, like your brother calling you a hippopotamus and your father saying you don't eat enough to keep a mouse alive.

All these problems are very common, but fortunately people come in all shapes and sizes. Our height and weight only become problems when we decide we don't like the way we are, especially when we get teased by people who are stupid enough to enjoy it. Such people are hurtful and play on our weaknesses. They make us feel helpless and inadequate.

Some people seem to eat huge amounts and stay very thin, and other people seem to eat very little and get fat. The trouble is that nobody knows exactly why this is. I always say that if you are putting on too much weight, then you are eating too much for YOU.

However, it doesn't seem as though you are very overweight at 52 kilos, as you can see from the charts of normal weights and heights of girls and boys that I have enclosed for you.

GIRLS

AGE	WEIGHT (kg)			HEIGHT (cm)		
	Low Normal	Middle	High Normal	Low Normal	Middle	High Normal
10 yrs	24	33	50	126	139	151
11 yrs	26	37	55	130	144	158
12 yrs	29	40	60	135	150	164
13 yrs	33	45	65	142	155	170
14 yrs	37	50	70	147	160	173
15 yrs	40	54	74	150	162	175
16 yrs	43	56	76	151	163	176
17 yrs	44	57	77	152	164	176
18 yrs	45	58	78	152	164	176

BOYS

AGE	WEIGHT (kg)			HEIGHT (cm)		
	Low Normal	Middle	High Normal	Low Normal	Middle	High Normal
10 yrs	24	31	46	126	139	151
11 yrs	25	34	52	130	143	157
12 yrs	28	38	57	134	147	163
13 yrs	30	43	65	140	155	171
14 yrs	35	49	72	146	162	179
15 yrs	39	55	80	153	169	185
16 yrs	44	60	85	158	173	188
17 yrs	48	64	88	161	175	190
18 yrs	51	66	90	165	176	190

Even if you are above or below this range, it doesn't mean anything is wrong with you. But if you are very much above or below, you may want to talk to someone about it.

It is quite common for girls of about your age to put on a bit of weight, and some people refer to this as 'puppy fat'. It is best to try not to get TOO fat, so that you will feel less self-conscious and enjoy doing things more. Also we know that fat grown-ups do have more health problems.

It has become fashionable for girls to think they should be very thin. Sometimes this goes too far and they don't know when to stop dieting. They THINK of themselves as fat even though they are extremely thin. This can lead to a problem called 'Anorexia Nervosa', where girls almost starve themselves to death.

I have enclosed some bits from letters that other people have written to me about these worries to show that you are not alone. I am also sending you some sensible eating hints which people have found useful.

Don't let your family get you down. Tell your brother that boys can just as easily become hippopotamuses as girls.

Yours sincerely

Chere Vainer

What people have said about being fat and thin
and some of my answers
Chere Vainer

I'm ten and a half stone and overweight, and have been since I was 10. I used to be called 'bubble, fatty, and big bum' and they said that when I ran 'there was an earth tremor'. I had a few friends, but even they used to call me names behind my back. I'm hoping to get to nine stone, and then I can go to discos and enjoy myself, but I am uncertain what my right weight should be. Can you help me please? I've asked my mum but she said it didn't matter to her whether I was overweight or not.

Answer: Your mum's right. You're still you, whatever your weight. But there are ways she could help you to lose a little. I'm sending you a diet sheet and a weight chart. Show them to her and try to plan some meals together. Also, try taking more exercise, like biking to school and back. Fill in the chart to help you see whether you've lost weight.

My problem is that I am slightly overweight. I have been since I was born, and it's not because I eat too much or don't take enough exercise. As I am tallish, my big stomach doesn't show so much, especially if I wear baggy clothes. I think that it is harder for males to diet than for females. Is this true?

Answer: You can't blame your sex. It's hard for everybody to lose weight. The main thing is that you must really want to. But it doesn't sound as if you have much of a problem if you eat a healthy diet and exercise!

I am overweight, though I don't eat too much. It's not really my weight that I think is the problem, more that I've got fat in all the wrong places. My legs look fat, especially my thighs, but everything else is all right. Worse is that all my friends are slim and pretty with feminine curves. I suppose if I was a boy, it would be different.

Answer: Fashion at the moment seems to see girls as slim, so of course girls want to be like the models that they see all the time on television. Don't care so much about what other people think. It's what you think of yourself that counts in the long run.

I think that I'm overweight because I eat too many sweets, but I can't stop eating them. I've tried eating the right kinds of food and lost a bit of weight, but not enough. I've tried exercise and my body ached, so I couldn't do any more. I've tried everything possible, but it just makes me more depressed. Last week I even bought some laxatives, but they didn't do anything. I've tried making myself sick, but it wouldn't come up.

Answer: Starving, or using laxatives, or making yourself sick is DANGEROUS. Doing these things can make you anorexic. Try eating sweets on only one day of the week. When you get the craving on other days, try a carrot or an apple instead. If you find yourself lured into sweet shops, then try asking for a packet of peanuts or raisins instead of sweets.

I am too thin. I was fat when I was young, but when I was about 10, I got thinner. I get called a lanky streak of bacon. How can I put on weight and be like Arnie Schwarzenegger?

Answer: Not everyone finds the Schwarzenegger look attractive – me for one. Some people do find it difficult to put on weight. It's probably just the way you're made. Look on the bright side. It's generally healthier to be thin than fat.

My weight problem is that I am too thin – especially in the legs. I've had this all my life, and so has my dad. People call me 'matchstick man' and ask if they can use me to light their cigarettes. I don't care so much now as I've taken up squash and have become bigger all over. I'd rather be thin than fat. Is this right?

Answer: There is no 'right' – thin or fat. It sounds as though the size you are is right for you – like your dad whom you inherited it from. Take no notice of people making jokes. It's their own lack of self-confidence that makes them do it. We ALL have our weak points, and for some people this is having to make jokes at other people's expense.

When I wear a tight skirt, I get teased and called 'fatty'. My best friend says I'm not, but I feel fat. When I look in the mirror it's depressing, and when I go shopping with my friend, all the nice things fit HER and are too small for ME. Why don't they make nice clothes in bigger sizes?

Answer: Shop around. Many shops do have clothes of larger sizes. In many ways you're lucky. I find the average sizes get sold out immediately.

I see myself as being different from other boys of the same age. In my eyes I am short and tubby, whereas everyone else seems tall and slim. When it comes to games I hate it. As we walk out to the sports field we have to pass the girls playing tennis. Most of them have already become mature, with breasts and things. I think that they look down on me. If one of them misses a tennis ball and laughs, I think they're laughing at me. The running track is worst. I can't run to save my life with my short fat legs, and people offer to buy me a clockwork tortoise to train with.

Answer: Fortunately we ARE all different from one another. But don't give up hope of getting taller and slimmer. When you reach puberty you may have the last laugh, as some boys grow a foot in a year.

What people have said about being too tall or too short

and some of my answers

Chere Vainer

I have the problem of being too small. It first came to prominence 2 years ago when I was 13. I am very keen on sport and tried for the school football team. My favourite position is central defence because I like tackling players, but I wasn't picked for the first few matches. The rest of the team got at me for being too small and causing us to lose our training matches because the ball was being lobbed over my head. I was dropped, but then the player who replaced me was so terrible that I got my place back.

Answer: As you've discovered, like many things in life, it's not your size that matters, it's the way that you use it.

I am too tall for my age. Some people think I'm 18 and call me 'lanky'.

Answer: Teenagers grow at different times, according to when they start and finish going through puberty. Soon all your friends will grow too, and you may want to be even taller!

My mother took me to see the doctor because I'm very small. He said that in my case it is because all my family are small. I've always been small and people call me 'shrimpy' and 'half-pint'. People say smoking stunts your growth, but I don't smoke. I've tried putting on platform heels, but they make me look stupid and are uncomfortable. It gets on my nerves when I'm buying clothes, and when I buy trousers I end up by cutting off half the legs.

Answer: Think of the advantages. You will save money when you're older as you'll be able to buy children's clothes. Think how much better being half-pint is than being quarter-pint. It's all comparative.

I think I am too tall and get depressed about it when people call me a beanpole. When I was 11, I was short, but now I've shot up and don't even fit properly into my bed. I don't like being tall, but my dad wants me to become a policeman, and if I was short they wouldn't have me. I suppose there are some advantages. At football you can see over everyone, and having long arms helps me to play basketball.

Answer: Get your parents to buy you a double bed so that you can fit your feet in. It'll come in useful later in life.

I'm called 'titch' and 'midget', and I think I'm small because I was born prematurely. When I came to secondary school we were shown around the first day and had a woodwork lesson, and I was embarrassed because I couldn't see over the top of the bench.

Because I'm small in height, it makes me feel small in character. I tend to be quiet, so people say I haven't got much confidence in myself. I always find it much easier talking to someone the same size as me.

Answer: Most people who are born prematurely will end up a perfectly normal height. Concentrate on all your good points, and this will make you feel more confident. Being more confident will make you FEEL bigger. Just because people are big doesn't mean that they are better.

I am so small that some people have suggested that I make a career of being a garden gnome.

Answer: Well don't – make a career out of being you, instead. Many of my friends who consider themselves 'small' develop a devastating list of cutting replies to this kind of remark. Try making some up, ready for next time.

I'm too small and I've had this problem since I was 5. I get teased and bullied, and cannot get into a '15' film without my birth certificate. When I'm in crowds, people look down on me and joke about it – even people I don't know. I laugh, but inside I get really upset. I can't wear fancy jeans because they don't fit me. People think that I'm younger than I am and I don't like that. I read about some children being small because they lack something called 'growth hormone'. Could this be my problem?

Answer: Growth hormone deficiency causes smallness in about 1 in 4,000 children. If you're worried, I would suggest you see your family doctor and discuss it.

Susie said I ought to keep a copy of the eating hints as she thinks I'm getting a bit fat myself. The cheek. It's not true.

ARE YOU WHAT YOU EAT?

Yes, you are!

SO WHAT DO YOU KNOW ABOUT WHAT YOU'RE EATING?

1. Which food is the most concentrated source of energy?
   (a) fat
   (b) protein
   (c) sugar
   (d) alcohol
   (e) dietary fibre

2. Which is the most easily available source of food energy?
   (a) vitamins
   (b) fat
   (c) carbohydrate
   (d) protein

3. How many portions of fruit and/or vegetables should you eat each day?
   (a) two
   (b) three
   (c) four
   (d) five

4. Taking large amounts of vitamin tablets:
   (a) Can replace meals?
   (b) Can be dangerous?
   (c) Is necessary in addition to a good diet?

5. Which of the following does not contain carbohydrate?
   (a) jam
   (b) bread
   (c) milk
   (d) butter

6. Which of these is not high in fat?
   (a) lean red meat
   (b) fruit
   (c) bread and potatoes
   (d) cheese
   (e) none of these

7. Which take-away foods are low in fat?
   (a) hamburger without chips
   (b) ham and cheese sandwich
   (c) fish and chips
   (d) none of these

Answers
1. a
2. c
3. d
4. b
5. d
6. b and c
7. d

So what is a good diet? Most magazines, parents, and health freaks go on and on about what you should and shouldn't eat. But no one really knows exactly what is right. What people do know is that HOW MUCH you eat of different foods is just as important as WHAT you eat. It's a matter of balance.

Throughout the world, people eat all sorts of different diets and most of them are OK as far as balance is concerned. But many people in many parts of the world are not getting ENOUGH food to give them enough energy to do what they need to do. This is what you ought to be concerned about: eating enough food to keep your energy up. You also need to get enough of some basic essentials (around 50 of them) to make sure you keep healthy.

No one food contains everything you need, so here are some very general 'goods' and 'bads'.

The basics of a good diet

» fruit, vegetables and salad: glut on these – eat at least 5 portions a day

» bread, cereals and potatoes: good fillers to stop you feeling hungry

» meat and dairy foods: choose carefully to avoid fat – fatty meat and hard cheeses are FULL of fat

» fish is fine

» oils, butter, margarine and spreads: less of these, and you'll eat less fat

» salt and sugar: you get all the salt you need per day just by eating bread and cereals, so you're probably eating far too much salt. There are natural sugars in fruit which are good and delicious. Stick with these and stay away from too much of the highly refined sugars (the stuff that looks like white sand, and that's in all the things you crave for! – the Mars bars, candy floss and chocolate cake).

Recommended Daily Amounts of Food Energy at Different Ages

AGE		ENERGY IN CALORIES
BOYS & MEN		
9–11 years		2280
12–14 years		2640
15–17 years		2880
18–54 years	lazing	2510
	moderately active	2900
	very active	3350
GIRLS & WOMEN		
9–11 years		2050
12–14 years		2150
15–17 years		2150
18–54 years	most occupations	2150
	very active	2500

FOOD		Calories
An apple		50
Bacon (2 rashers)		160
A banana		80
Baked beans	– 1 portion	150
A biscuit	– chocolate	50
	– wafer	100
	– custard cream	60
Bread	– 1 slice	100
Bread/butter/jam		250
Butter (30 gm)		210
Cakes	– choc roll	120
	– Chelsea bun	255
	– doughnut	125
	– apple pie	210
	– cream slice	250
	– jam tart	105
A carrot		20
Cereal	– 1 portion	130
Chicken nuggets	– 1 portion	270
Chips	– 1 portion	440
Chocolate bar		315
Crisps	– 1 packet	135
Cucumber	– 1 portion	12
Drinks	– Coca-Cola	130
	– diet Pepsi	0
	– fruit drinks	85
	– milk shakes	365
	– tea (milk and sugar)	40
Fish	– 1 portion	460
Hamburgers	– Big Mac	555
	– Standard	250
Ice cream	– a choc ice	130
	– a cone	100
An ice lolly		55
A lamb chop		175
Milk	– 1 pint	370
Milk	– 1 pint skimmed	200
An orange		50

```
A pizza         10" thin & crispy
                cheese and tomato        610
                10" deep pan pepperoni  1585!
A potato        - jacket                  170
                - jacket plus butter      255
Sausages        - 2 pork                  370
Steaks          - 1 lean portion          300
A tangerine                                20
A yoghurt       - plain                    75
                - fruit                   130
```

Wednesday 25th September Asked Cills to the pictures. Help!
She said, 'YES'. Suddenly came all over nervous.

Sunday 29th September Not going to wash my hands for a week.
Was holding Cills' for the last 20 minutes of the film. SUCCESS AT LAST!
Can't even remember what film was about.

15 **Wart-Hogs** and **Odious Odours** from **Orifices**

Tuesday 1st October Teachers are like parents – never practise what they preach. Today was Smelly Breath Rogers telling us about hygiene: washing in our cracks, changing our knickers every day (already worried the Y-fronts Mum buys me are making my balls dry up before I've even had a chance to try them out), using deodorants, and the evils of nose picking, bum scratching, farting and burping.

Everyone knows what HE's eaten for breakfast, what fags he smokes, and which beer he drinks for lunch, from 10 smelly feet away. But today he broke his all-time record by burping, scratching his bum and farting (silent killer type) all at the same time, and then looking at Sam accusingly.

Totally polluting smell of stale sweat in changing room at school, tinged with unwashed feet or, as old Will S. would have it, 'The rankest compound of villainest smell that ever offended nostrils' (*The Merry Wives of Windsor*), hangs around in spite of Mr Rogers's talk and his leaflet on 'Keeping It Clean'.

Had to write on 'What Makes People Smell' for homework. Supposed to stimulate our interest in the subject! Nearly did myself in getting library copy of the *Oxford Medical Textbook* off top shelf. It said (after translation via my medical dictionary) that our smells come from special glands called 'aprocrine glands' that are in our armpits, around our nipples (mine are not up to much), and around our dicks and bum hole. They don't start working till puberty, and then produce stuff which is a mixture of dead cells and greasy substances – ugh. This stuff is all decomposed by bacteria that normally live on the surface of the skin, and this makes chemicals which give us our body odours – the dreaded BO.

In animals this smelly stuff is important for marking out territorial areas. Can't imagine anyone marking out our changing room as an important territorial area. Aprocrine glands and their smells are a kind of sexual organ – so why aren't I turned on by Cills's armpit smells then? If I get close enough, then maybe I will be?

Seems that moths might be, though. There are these things called 'pheromones', which are just small molecules of chemicals floating around in the air like radio waves, giving us messages via our noses. They're like smells, but we don't even notice them, except that they may alter our behaviour. 'A female moth', the textbook said, 'can release enough of a chemical called 'bombykol' all at once to attract a trillion males from miles around, in an instant.'

Desperate for a bottle of the human male equivalent – there'd be no stopping me then.

Apparently deodorants work by killing off the bacteria living on our skin. But they're knocking off all those lovely pheromones too and doing away with lots of smelly, sexy, unconscious messages to the opposite sex. Also, what you eat, like garlic, comes out in these aprocrine glands as well.

Then there's the sweat glands themselves – called 'eccrine glands' – with about 3 to 4 million of them all over our bodies, including our hands and face. On a normal day they produce about 500 cubic centimetres of sweat, but full blast they can manage up to 3 or 4 litres an hour. Sounds more like 'bathed in sweat' than just 'dripping with'.

It also said that 'man' (what about 'woman' – somebody should mention sexism and political correctness to these doc authors) uses the evaporation of sweat from our skin to keep us cool, unlike other animals, which use insulation against heat, or panting when they get too hot. Emotion and anxiety also make us sweat. (Telling me – when I finally managed to hold Cills's hand last week in the cinema, mine must have felt like a wet sponge. Scares me that every time she comes near, my brain slips out of gear and I can't think what to say.)

Hate getting sweaty hands and feet, and they don't seem to be the only places – as my underpants keep falling to pieces. Maybe it's because they just can't stand the strain of what's inside. Sally is always going on about how I pong – doesn't seem to understand it's all natural and to do with the breakdown of my skin and clothes.

Got top marks for my PSHE. Wouldn't have expected less. Randy Joe found an article called 'Favourite Words', about how some docs had asked a hundred children what their favourite words were for dicks and vaginas. It was wasted on Mr Rogers, who said Joe had a dirty mind. Luckily I have a dirty mind, like the docs who asked the questions, so Joe gave it to me.

Favourite words for **penis**:

dick, willy, cock, knob, knob end, winkle, penis, dinkle, willie warbler, twinkle, ding-a-ling, my body, diggle, big worm, prick, tail, wotsit, privates, winkler, dilly dat, little man, hosepipe, nudger, tinkle, wedding tackle

Favourite words for **vagina**:

fanny, vagina, pinkie, vag, cunt, tweet, fluffy bit, tummy, foo foo, no willie, luly, front bottom, special tummy, crumpet, tuppeny, ninny, foo, cavern, pocket, channel tunnel, wee wee, twinkle, private

Favourite words for **anus**:
bum, bottom, arse, backside, arse hole, back passage

Favourite words for **testicles**:
balls, testicles, goolies, privates, nuts, rugby balls, bollocks

Favourite words for **shitting**:
poohs, toilet, loo, number two, plops, sit down, do a soggy, dump pooh
cheese, bobs, big ones, cack, big toilet, go bum, shit, mud, kaka, shite,
popper, big job

Favourite words for **passing wind**:
fart, pardon, wind, blow off, fluffed, permped, bum burp, pop off, rude
noise, trump, pass wind, done one, cracked a nut, let polly out, bottom
noise, whiffed, bottom spoke, prout, guff, windy pops

Favourite words for **peeing**:
wee wee, toilet, loo, widdle, bog, pee pee, piss, aunty Jane

Favourite words for **vomiting**:
sick, puke, throw up, chuck, chunder, hurl, barf, blow chunks

Not much about most of these words in my medical dictionary, though.

Wednesday 2nd October Got jumped on in the pool today. Nearly
drowned. What a way to go – in other people's chlorinated pee. Mr
Rogers was supervising, and as he fished me out said I should've been
more careful as drowning is the third most common way of kids dying,
after car accidents and burns, and it is still a lot more likely than me
dying of Aids. Objected to this speculation on my future sex life. Anyhow
survived, with stinging eyes – result of the pee/chlorine mixture, though

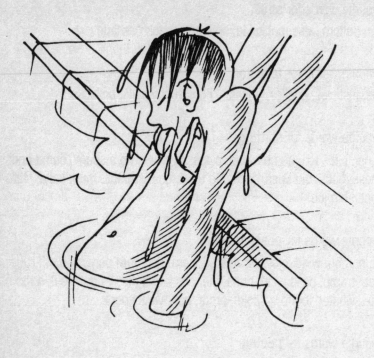

not guilty of this mix myself this time. In Mr Rogers's mind, the pool is a viral and fungal paradise, 'a new hazard at every footstep,' he said with relish.

Probably true though, cos each time I've caught athletes' foot it's been at the pool, in the changing room or in the showers. Don't think it's serious, just very embarrassing, especially trying to get your shoe off to rub the terrible itch between your toes, hoping nobody will see you. Mum always gives me the same old lecture about drying properly between my toes (too old for 'This little piggy went to market') and about not wearing my comfy smelly trainers.

Rather have smelly feet with skin dropping off than wear black leathers, so I'm still changing my shoes in the garage. When the smell gets too bad, Mum stuffs my clean socks with a tin of powder and a tube of cream. I'm a walking pharmacy – Mycil, Daktarin, Myocota – you name 'em, I've tried 'em.

Friday 4th October Ugh – now Susie's got the dreaded warts. They've sprouted on her thumb. Think they look horrendous and dirty. Wonder if it's cos she sucks her thumb? Hope I don't catch them. It would be the end of holding hands with Cills – just when I've made a sweaty start. Want to ask her out again but don't know where to take her.

Saturday 5th October Susie's becoming a real toady wart-hog. Now she's got them on her feet too. Thought you got verrucas on your feet, but turns out that's just another name for warts which grow inwards on your soles cos of pressure. Susie's busy painting her feet with stuff called 'salicylic acid' from the chemist. Says it kills off the warty skin and then YOU have to scrape the dead skin off. Told Susie if she scraped too hard there'd be nothing left of her.

Don't much fancy having a bath after her – not that I have one often. At least now she's got something other than her weight to worry about.

Sunday 6th October Three of Susie's friends came to 'play'. Tea consisted of wart talk. Put right off my egg and toast.

Her friend Kate said you had to get hold of a piece of raw steak, rub it on the wart, and bury it. Trouble was when she did it, her dog kept digging it up and eating it. Her mum said to use Pedigree Chum next time, as it was cheaper, and anyhow her warts had spread. Now she was trying her gran's recipe – wiping it with the juice of a dandelion stalk, and putting the broken dandelion onto the thorn of a rose bush. With luck, when it died, her wart would fall off. If it didn't, her gran's next best remedy was attending three funerals, and saying each time, as the funeral bells were ringing, 'Please take my warts with you'.

Mum said that when she was young (yonks ago), you had to spit on your warty hands every morning. She tried it and it didn't work, but she kept forgetting to do it anyhow.

Mary said Susie could try peeing on her hands, but I suggested swimming in the local pool might have the same effect.

Monday 7th October Dead worried. Something is growing on my knee. No one's hand has been there recently, but I'm spitting on it every hour, just in case. Keep missing but helps clean my shoes.

Friday 11th October Mum's taking Susie to some weirdo called 'a podiatrist' tomorrow to have her verrucas fixed. Didn't explain to Mum about my knee, but said I would come too, to keep them company.

Saturday 12th October A podiatrist turns out to be a 'foot specialist' – must be smelly work if my feet are anything to go by. She said the spot on my knee wasn't a wart, just a pimple, and would get better if I stopped messing with it. Checked my feet, and gave me a lecture on how important it is to have well-fitting shoes. Otherwise you can get corns and callouses caused by rubbing from bad-fitting shoes.

When it came to Susie's feet (don't know how she could stand getting close to THEM), she got quite excited and started on a new lecture about how warts, whether on the hands or the feet, ARE catching. They happen when wart viruses (and apparently there are loads of different kinds) get into cracks or cuts in our skin. As with my athletes' foot, swimming baths and changing rooms are common places to get infections. Happen most in children aged 12 to 16, but some children NEVER get them, some get just the odd one, and some get lots and lots. No one knows why (seems to be a lot that people don't know about when it comes down to it).

Over half of the warts disappear in 2 years, even if you do nothing about them. Probably explains why all that digging meat into the ground, and going to funerals, SEEMS to work. If you use any of the medical treatments, like salicylic acid, then three-quarters will clear up in 3 months, which seems a bit better. For the ones that don't go away with this treatment, then burning, freezing or scraping away the dead skin can help.

Seemed to make Susie feel happier, though she had expected hers to go away overnight after she had tried the acid, and she didn't fancy the bits about burning or freezing. The foot doc said Susie can go swimming as long as she wears a plaster to cover her verrucas.

Sunday 13th October Bits of Susie's dead skin on the bathroom floor this morning. Used downstairs bog to pick my nose in instead. She's asked Mum if she could have her tummy button pierced today. Not sure about all this piercing stuff, reckon you could get Aids from it. Checked www.doctorann.org – who's done a whole quiz on it and it sounded dead horrid.

Tooth
Piercing,
Body
Piercing

Tuesday 22nd October Randy Joe took Cills to the cinema again last night. Told me today, didn't he? Hate, hate, even if he didn't get anywhere with her – real little Britney Spears, he said. Anyhow his acne's worse than mine and he spends all his pocket money on girlie magazines. Reckon he needs a heart transplant cos he ain't got one. Told him last time I got near Cills at the cinema, her breath smelt a bit. Wish I hadn't – he'll probably tell her.

Read this thing about someone in Minnesota, USA, who kissed 8,000 people in 8 hours, which is kissing 1 person every 3.6 seconds. In Israel 2 people kissed each other for 30 hours and 45 minutes. Yuck – you can have too much of a good thing.

Wednesday 23rd October Mum took us to new dentist. Said we were lucky to find one who still worked for the National Health Service, and would give us our treatment free if we were under 18. In some places they're rarer than hen's teeth nowadays…ha, ha.

Susie had this final fitting for her brace, so Mum suddenly had to remember me too, didn't she? Was scared stiff of my old dentist, who would pin me to the chair and be furious if I so much as screamed occasionally. She went bankrupt. Served her right. Don't know why they don't replace dentists with robots, like the ones that build cars.

Dentists are bigger liars than politicians. They say they won't hurt, but you come out in agony, with lips feeling the size of a blue baboon's bum. But some have traces of being human – like this new one. He's nice – has space gadgets and makes jokes all the time. With my mouth full of bits of metal, it's easier to laugh than answer stupid questions. Says it's boring dealing with rotten teeth every day, just cos people can't be bothered to clean them. Gave me a leaflet to read while he was poking around in Susie's mouth. Took an extra leaflet for bad breath Cills. I know it'll piss her off but I don't care. Anybody who goes out with Randy Joe has to be a slag.

GOOD TEETH, GOOD LOOKS

Good teeth, bad teeth – it's not down to luck

Remember, neglect your teeth and they soon start to look dingy. Worse still, they can decay and cause pain. And they can also create an unpleasant smell and taste in your mouth.

This leaflet will help you get to know what's good for your teeth and what's bad for them. You should ask your dentist for any further advice and practical assistance you need.

Despite what you may have heard, it's not chance that will help you keep your teeth and your looks. It's knowing what to do and then doing it.

ENEMIES

'Tooth decay' ✗

What happens is that sugar and bacteria in the mouth get together and make an acid. This acid attacks the tooth enamel first, and then deeper. And that can hurt! To your teeth, sugar is enemy No.1.

Sugar ✗

You don't need it. Your teeth hate it. And it is worst if you're forever munching sweet things and having fizzy drinks between meals. That's how most damage is done. If you do like your sweets and cola, cut them down to just after meals.

Plaque ✗

We've all got it. Run your tongue round your teeth and you'll feel a furry, glue-like substance. That's 'plaque'. But don't worry. It's how long plaque stays at any one time and is allowed to build up that matters. That's why brushing is so important. The bacteria in plaque cause gum disease – the earliest sign of this is that your gums bleed when they are brushed. In the end, the gum and bone supporting the teeth may be destroyed, causing the teeth to become loose and to fall out.

Bleeding gums ✗

There's nothing natural about your gums bleeding – even if they don't hurt. And if you don't brush your teeth, or floss them, often enough, you may start seeing blood on your toothbrush. Should this happen, then (surprisingly perhaps!) you really should start brushing your teeth more frequently. And if that doesn't put things right, see your dentist.

FRIENDS

Your toothbrush, naturally ✓

Almost certainly you already brush your teeth, but do you do it properly? It isn't easy. The difficult part is to remove plaque where the gums meet the teeth. Your dentist will show you exactly where to brush and how to do it.

Regular brushing is important too. You do your hair every day – why not do your teeth every day?

Flossing ✓

Dental floss is white cotton-like stuff that comes in a thin string which your pull backwards and forwards in the cracks between your teeth to help get the bits of food out. You can get it from your chemist. Like brushing your teeth, you should try and floss in the cracks between your teeth at least once a day.

Fluoride ✓

Use a fluoride toothpaste. Fluoride is a naturally occurring substance which is present in small quantities in many foods – such as tea or fish – as well as in water. It unites with tooth enamel and makes teeth stronger, less likely to decay. But most of us don't get enough of it from natural sources, so we need it in toothpaste.

Try something tasty and safe between meals ✓

Why sweets anyway? Try nuts, fruit, carrots or celery. Look around and you'll find many enjoyable tasty bites that won't harm your teeth.

THE DENTIST

A friend indeed!

Don't for a minute think that your dentist is there only to drill, fill or extract. In fact, regular visits could mean he or she never has to do those things for you! Your dentist will check your teeth carefully and care for them when necessary and give you all the advice you need about looking after them between visits.

Look on your dentist as someone who will help you KEEP your teeth. And your looks.

Cor! What kind of patronizing git wrote that?

Had to have a filling, and the worst bit was when he crammed cotton-wool pads, a sucker thing, and a drill into my mouth all at the same time. Thought I was going to drown in my own spit – what a way to go, worse than chlorinated pee.

Meanwhile dentist burbled on about how your teeth need ONE really good, thorough brush every day, with any toothbrush and (most important) with FLUORIDATED toothpaste. He reckoned that if everybody did this – or if the government fluoridated all drinking water, like they do in Moscow, New York, Birmingham, Dublin and Sydney; and if people gave up eating sweets and other sugary things all the time, and just ate them occasionally, say on Wednesdays and Saturdays – then teeth problems would almost disappear and he could retire. The average English schoolchild eats 118 grams of sugar EVERY day. This sugar is turned into acid by bugs in our mouths and starts eating into the enamel of our teeth within a few seconds – ugggghhh!

Went on about how most old people have NO teeth of their own – not one! (Gran's like this. She keeps all her spare false teeth in a plastic bag in her bathroom cupboard.) About half of children aged 15 have had at least ONE filling (and now I'm one of them). Then gave me this lecture about tooth brushing – about using small backwards and forwards scrubbing movements, gently all over all my teeth, inside and out, and particularly where my teeth go into the gum. OK, mmmmm enoouugghh of daaat, daaanks.

At least I'm not 'brace faced' like Susie, who's got to wear this cage at night – 'for your own good', as Mum said – cos the front teeth on her top jaw are all crooked and stick out, and there is a big gap between them (like the bride of Dracula) which she can't clean with a normal toothbrush.

Friday 25th October Sssusie sssays that it'sss like having ssseventeen sssets of teeth. Ssshe ssspeaks like thisss all the time.

Saturday 26th October Susie's nagging Mum for compensation over her brace. Says if Mum won't let her have her tummy button pierced, at least she could let her have her ears pierced. Two of her friends at school have just done each other's – with a needle which they tried to 'sterilize' by holding it over a candle. Mum was HORRIFIED. Said you can get all sorts of infections that way – like Aids and hepatitis. Mum said she'd had hers done when she was 20, but if Susie really wanted hers done now, she must go somewhere licensed where they'd use proper sterilized packs.

Suppose Mum should be grateful that it's only her ears Susie wants done, as nipple, lip and tongue piercing is all the rage. I'll ask Cills what she thinks, as she's had her tummy pierced. Sounds fantastically painful. Reckon Randy Joe should have his ego extension pierced. That would be even more painful, which would serve him right.

My older sister Sal, as usual, is a real expert. Has five in one ear alone and a nose ring. But she agrees it's best to have them done properly in a shop, even if it does cost. She's had hers done at different times, and the best one was when her current boyfriend gave her nine-carat gold sleepers to put in. The cheap sleepers she'd used before had always made her ears all pussy. Sal said it was really important to keep the sleepers in for a whole month, and that Susie would need to keep the ear lobes very clean, and to turn her sleepers regularly.

None of this seems to have put Susie off. Mum's given in and she's having them done next week – funny how the youngest in the family always gets everything they want.

Days
off
School
Thinking I'm Dying

Monday 4th November Street firework party was ruined. I sometimes think it's a pity Guy Fawkes didn't manage to blow up the Houses of Parliament and himself too.

Nick got blown up last night – both by a rocket and by his parents, who had to take him to the local hospital to have the burns on his face treated. Told him there that he'd got 'second degree burns', which (from my dictionary) means he's got blisters, red streaking and oozing of the skin, with a lot of pain. Nick said they'd put this special non-stick dressing on and told him he might need a skin graft.

MY own mistake was to pick up a used sparkler before it had cooled down – what a loser. Luckily Mum knew first-aid and immediately made me put my hand into cold water for 5 minutes. Said this cooled the burn and stopped too many of my cells from getting killed off. Certainly helped the pain. Mum said that burns like Nick's had to be treated immediately by a doctor cos otherwise they could become infected or cause worse scarring. To begin with, my burn hurt like hell, but Mum said that was OK cos with very deep burns the nerves get damaged and there isn't so much pain. Well that's OK, then.

This morning I'd a massive great long blister (luckily across my left hand), which I want to pop, but Mum won't let me as she says the skin on the blister is protecting the damaged cells underneath from infection. Not as bad as my sunburn in the summer, though. Got a massive headache and felt wobbly at dinner, so went to bed early and can hardly write this.

Thursday 7th November Tried to get dressed this morning but gave up. Curled up on the sofa downstairs instead and had just got comfy, with the heater on, when Mum walked in and flared up cos I wasn't ready for school. Explained how terrible I felt but she wouldn't listen, and said that if I was really ill, I had to go back to bed. Thought I was putting it on, didn't she? But took my temperature and changed her mind when she saw it was 39.5 degrees centigrade. It's funny. Although it was up 2.5 degrees, I actually felt dead cold and shivery. Wonder how high my temperature can go? Bet I would die after about 45 degrees...feel as if I'm on my way there now.

Mum rang the doctor, who came to see me at home as I seemed so sick. Said it was probably JUST flu and caused by a virus and I'd be

better in 3 or 4 days. Reckoned there was no treatment except for me to stay in bed if I felt like it, have lots of clear drinks, and take paracetamol every 4 to 6 hours. Said the paracetamol would bring my temperature down and help my headache. If I die, it'll be all her fault.

Told her about the headaches I've been having, like the one when Mum and Dad were having their 'discussions'. So she looked in the back of my eyes with a light – like they did at the hospital when I had my accident. Told me it wasn't a brain tumour or meningitis, or anything else seriously wrong, which I'm glad about, as I'd been worrying. Said if it was meningitis, it would hurt to bend my neck and I'd be much iller.

This doc was a bit nosy about my life at school and at home, but said there are lots of causes for headaches, like being tense, or not being very well, but usually they go away without anyone knowing what caused them. If it was migraine, she said, the headache would've been on one side, and I'd be getting funny lines across my eyesight before the headache starts. Said it runs in families, but Mum says no one in MY family has it.

The doc said that if ever I was worried about things, I could come and talk to her. Didn't have to bring Mum or Dad along, and she would treat anything that I said as 'confidential'. I didn't understand what 'confidential' meant, so she explained that if I didn't want her to, she wouldn't tell anything I said to anyone else, including my parents, and that it didn't matter that I wasn't 16 years old yet. Sounds OK to me.

After she left, I went from being shivery to being all hot and soaked in sweat. Could have fried an egg on me, I reckon. Flung all my bedclothes off, and told Mum I wanted to go easy on the paracetamol cos I'd read somewhere that having a bit of a temperature may help to kill off the infection. Took one though, just to help my throbbing headache. Can't write any more. Hurts too much.

Friday 8th November Dying, though did manage a few games on my Playstation. Nobody cares. They'll be sorry when it's too late, except Mum, who's the best nurse anyone could have. My thermometer says 40 degrees.

Saturday 9th November Didn't die and temperature down to 38.5. Susie's going spare cos one of her pierced ears has gone pussy. Told her the rest of her would probably follow. Mum told her to keep bathing it with the lotion they gave her and it would clear up OK.

Randy Joe's had his tongue pierced! Possibly less painful than the latest place I had in mind for him, alas. Why hasn't Cills rung up to find out if I'm dead or not?

Monday 11th November Temperature 37.0 degrees – normal again. Susie's ill now. Came home early, but wouldn't tell me what was wrong, but after a bit of third degree admitted it was her period pains. Now it's official she's started.

Feeling better today, but at first it was horrible. Felt so ill. My head felt as if it was going to burst, couldn't sleep, and the nights went so slowly it was just a matter of waiting for morning. Ached all over and was hot, but my joints were freezing. Mum's very grumpy about us being home all the time, maybe cos she can't go to work, but I've diagnosed flu and told her to take paracetamol and go to bed.

Spent part of the day watching baby programmes, *Neighbours*, gratuitous violence, and a programme on the human brain. Apparently some Russian writer called Turgenev had the heaviest brain ever recorded. They'd cut him up and his brain had weighed in at 2,012 grams, whereas an average man's brain is 1,410 grams. Wonder if I could have a transplant from someone real brainy like that Hawking bloke, or maybe a gene transplant would be better! At least it said that my brain is 10 times the size of a gorilla's, even though the hairy beast weighs 3 or 4 times more than even my Mum. Found out some more facts about my beautiful bod, like it holds 5 litres of blood, and my heart pumps 90 cubic centimetres at every beat – so normally about 5 litres, or the complete amount of blood in my body, every minute. This can go up to 30 litres (all my blood being pumped around my body 6 times in a minute) during hard exercise – not often in my case! More likely to all get pumped to some other part of me!

Other facts about my heart are: it weighs about 260 grams and the most normal rate for it to beat at is 70–75 beats a minute, but can go very rapidly from 45 beats per minute when resting to 200 beats during exercise. The heart is made up of 200,000,000,000 cells – amazing when you think that my whole bod started off as just 2 cells.

There are 96,560 kilometres of arteries, veins and blood capillaries in the human body, through which all this blood travels. Also learnt from TV that there are 1,000,000,000,000 nerve cells in our brain, and after we are 18 we lose a thousand of these every day. (Wonder whose job it is counting all these cells and measuring how long all the blood vessels are?) Our kidneys filter 90 litres of blood per day, which means that all the blood in our body is filtered 17 times every 24 hours, but we only produce about 2 litres of pee each day.

Susie keeps barging into my room to see what I'm doing. Wish she'd knock. Could be real embarrassing. She's bored, but I wanted her to buzz off, till she told me I'd missed another sex talk at school. Knows my weak spots, doesn't she? Sudden change of interest on my part. Luckily she'd brought home a leaflet.

YOU CAN SAY 'NO!'

YOUR BODY BELONGS TO *YOU*

Sometimes you can know someone for a long time and like them a lot, and then they'll start to do things you don't like at all. Perhaps they'll start touching you in a way that seems strange to you, but since you like the person and he's always been nice to you, you don't like to ask him to stop. But you can and you should. Because you don't have to let anyone touch you in a way you don't like, even if it's an adult you've always got on well with. Or even if it's someone in your own family. Or a neighbour.

STRANGERS

You've probably been told many times not to take sweets from strangers, or get into a car with someone you don't know, because they might do bad things to you. But people we know well can also do bad things to us, by making us believe they are not bad.

IT'S NOT SPECIAL TO BE SEXUALLY ABUSED!

A person might tell you that what he feels about you is something very special, and that you must keep it secret because other people would not understand. And perhaps he makes you feel very special. However, this happens to many girls and boys, and it is not special.

IT'S UNFAIR IF A GROWN-UP MAKES YOU DO THINGS YOU DON'T UNDERSTAND

In fact, the grown-up (or sometimes it's a teenager) is being very unfair, because he is bigger than you and knows more about everything. So he can easily get you to do things you don't really want to. So that later on, when you do understand, you'll feel very angry. I'm saying 'he' all the time, but it can sometimes be a woman.

FIND SOMEONE WHO CAN HELP YOU

If this happens to you and you can't get the person to stop bothering you and you can't keep out of his way, you should tell someone you think will help you – a schoolteacher, or your mother, or an older sister, or a policewoman, for instance. If you tell one person and they don't believe you, or are too frightened to help you, then try someone else, and keep trying till you find someone who will help you.

Also, tell your friends, so that they can stay away from that person too, and their parents can help.

DON'T BE BULLIED

If one of your friends tells you about someone bothering her, then try to help her in every way you can, because it's horrible to be alone with a problem like this. You start thinking things, like 'There must be something wrong with me or he wouldn't have done that'. But in fact there's nothing wrong with you at all. You're not the problem. The person doing it to you is doing wrong.

YOU ARE NOT TO BLAME

It is frightening when something like this happens, but you can be absolutely sure it's all right to say 'No!' and you can be sure, too, that it's not your fault. It's nothing you've done which made this person behave in the way he did. He has probably done it to other children, and he will certainly go on doing it if he is not stopped. We don't like telling tales, but this is different. If you tell people, he can be stopped.

REMEMBER, IT'S YOUR BODY AND YOU CAN SAY 'NO!'. YOU CAN RING CHILDLINE ON 0800 1111, WHERE THEY TREAT ANYTHING THAT YOU SAY AS ABSOLUTELY SECRET.

Susie said she reckoned that the talk was because of what happened to one of her friends called Jane. She's meant to have only told Susie, though. About a week ago, when Jane was on her way home, a car stopped and a man she knew as a friend of her parents asked her the way to the local superstore. He pretended he didn't understand her directions and said could she just hop in and guide him. Susie said Jane had always been a real dumbo – the type that would be kind to Godzilla if she met him in the street – and she got in. He started putting his hand up her skirt, and saying dirty things about touching his dick. Jane got very angry and began screaming, so he became all friendly and nice again, and tried to bribe her with sweets not to say anything. He said it had to be THEIR special secret, and that they would both get into terrible trouble if anyone found out.

Jane didn't know what to do cos she thought her mum would be furious, but she told her all the same. Her mum said it wasn't Jane's fault, it was all the man's, which made her feel much better. Her mum must've done something about it, cos a couple of days later, when Jane was less upset, her mum said that the man had agreed to have some special treatment, and was going to move far away to another town.

Susie said the sex talk at school was what Mum and Dad had said a million times already about not accepting lifts or presents of any kind from strangers, and even perhaps being a bit careful of friends! Sometimes it's real difficult to tell the difference between when people are just being nice to you, and hugging or kissing, and when somebody is trying to do something nasty to you. Mum says the best thing is being aware that it might happen. And if it does, saying 'NO' and meaning it, and saying it with your whole body – pushing away, getting angry (instead of being frozen with fear), and ALWAYS telling someone. Best of all is not getting into situations that you don't know how to get out of, though some things, like flashers in churches and other pervs, are difficult to avoid.

Susie said she is going to learn self-defence. Can't exactly see her chopping someone in half with a single blow, but said I thought it was a good idea as long as she didn't practise on me.

The women of my family ALL into period problems. Silence falls as Dad or me approach. Told Dad I'd try and find us an all-man problem – but could only come up with CDS, which is much more frequent than the monthlies and stands for Cills Deprivation Syndrome.

Tuesday 12th November Feel mixed about going back to school. Getting really bored being at home, but have loads of work to catch up with when I get back. Bet no one believes I've been ill. None of my mates have been to see me.

Wednesday 13th November Back to school and good to see my friends again, but now Sam's away with flu. Seems it's going round. Had to have a supply teacher for games, as Mr Jones has it too. Hope the supply teacher gets something worse. He thought I was skiving when I said I felt too tired to play football.

Thursday 14th November Borrowed this really funny book which must've been through a million people's hands before me cos it was so battered. It was called *Man's Best Friend*, all about dicks with a life of their own. Might lend it to Cills. Back on her again.

Tests in maths and biology next week. Was worried that I might have missed some stuff for them while I was ill, but luckily the first thing we got taught in maths today was about revising and how not to get stressed. Last year, when I was doing some tests about the human body, I didn't know where to start revising. Thought I had to learn the name of every bone in the body. Another problem is that I never feel I have time to do all the questions.

Now what I'm doing is looking at everything I'm meant to cover, sorting it out into different topics, and making a timetable so that I can cover everything at least a bit, in the time I've got, instead of getting hung up on only doing one thing really thoroughly.

Another thing we were told was that we can only concentrate for so long, so it is best to work for an hour and then have a break – watch telly, play on my Playstation, whatever.

Wednesday 20th November Worried – I hate tests.

Thursday 21st November Wiped out. Two tests today. In first one, completely forgot what the teachers said about timing. Only completed 14 out of 20 questions in the maths, as I got stuck on the third one and wasted lots of time. Didn't help finding out that Sam found the last 6 questions dead easy.

Did better in biology. There were 10 questions to do in 2 hours. First I read them all carefully for 10 minutes so that I understood what they were about, and then really concentrated on answering each question for 10 minutes only. That left 10 minutes at the end for my terrible spelling.

18

Four **Eyes**
with Pebbles on

Monday 25th November Another bad day. Mrs Smellie moved me to the front of the class – said I was 'not concentrating'. Was concentrating, but was busy copying out Sam's homework on something that I'd missed when I had flu. Made me abandon my desk at the back, specially chosen to be out of teacher's view. So furious and embarrassed, stomped to the front, clutching all my gear. Dropped latest copy of *Practical Photography* as I passed Cills and it fell open at a page revealing a woman with all her bits showing. Blushed to the roots of my acned hair follicles, insisting that the magazine had been bought for photographic purposes only. Could've killed Cills who muttered, 'Me thinks he doth protest too much' (had Shakespeare to thank for that one).

When I'd stopped sulking, suddenly noticed that I could ACTUALLY READ what Mrs Smellie had written on the blackboard without screwing up my eyes or copying off my neighbour. This may improve my work, but am I going blind?

Tuesday 26th November Another puncture. Found I'd left the top off the tube of rubber solution, which had dried up. Unsuccessfully tried to blame Susie. Took bus to school and nearly got on the wrong one, as I could only see the number when it was close. Even more worried about going blind (though Dad had told me that playing with myself didn't do that). Will I have to wear glasses, like Dad? Can't stand even thinking about it – too grim.

Wednesday 27th November Came top in biology. Told Cills it was all the practical experience I had had. My maths – I'm not letting on, but Raj came top. Some of the brainiest and hardest people in our class are either Asian or West Indian and usually the girls too.

Trouble at home. Bent all the teaspoons trying to lever off my tyre. Susie turned out to be an expert puncture mender and said she'd do it for me when she got back from her self-defence class. Tried offering her 50p per puncture for the future, but she negotiated £1.00. Bet she becomes a union boss when she grows up, and growing up she certainly seems to be.

Looked in the mirror to try and imagine what I would look like with pebble glasses. Would hide some of the zits – or might magnify them? Shock horror!

Monday 2nd December Got a note today for Mum about an eye test at school next week. Apparently they do one every 2 or 3 years. First note I haven't left in my pocket to block up the washing machine for ages (Mum loves me and Sal for this). Bit worried about the eye test in case I fail and really do need glasses, especially as on the way home Sam called Eddie Marley 'Four Eyes'. Eddie said, 'Four eyes are better than two, man,' and when someone else said, 'What's it like walking around with double glazing?', all he said was, 'I have the best – dey are Everest!' Doesn't seem to worry him, but I kept quiet.

Monday 9th December Day of the TEST. Kept trying to see if I could read the bus numbers on the way to school, but no way, they were just a blur in the distance. Best thing was that the eye test was during my PE lesson. Unlike at lunchtime, everyone was trying to get to the BACK of the queue, so as to miss as much school as poss. School nurse, Hazel Chops, who looks ancient and must have had at least 18 children (perhaps that's why they chose her?), turned a cold eye on us all, which silenced us like a laser beam.

My turn came at last. Stood in front of the chart, which they had put about 5 miles away, and could only read to the third line before the letters blurred out. Felt real panicky, like when I know I am going to fail an exam. Tried to remember the letters from the last time I had had the test, but couldn't. Asked old Guzzler Guts Gary (whose breath not only kills at 40 feet, but who'll do almost anything for a bribe of a sweet – hence the rotten teeth and noxious breath) to read the letters on the chart and whisper them to me. Alas, even HIS greed grew dim under the school nurse's gaze. What a lightweight. So failed miserably.

Hazel Chops turned out to be nice, even if she was a bit crinkly. Realized how sad I was and said it wasn't a question of 'failing' but of not being able to see normally. Also said not to worry, she was sure there was nothing seriously wrong and probably I just needed glasses…but that I should see an optician who would test my eyes more thoroughly. Told her how much I hated the idea of wearing glasses, and then noticed that she was wearing them, which made me feel dead embarrassed. She explained that at my age, about 1 in 5 children wear glasses, and by her age nearly everyone does. So there's no harm in getting used to them early, and anyway I might be able to have contact lenses. This made me feel a bit better – but still not wild about the idea.

Passed the colour test though, where they make you read a whole lot of numbers made up of different coloured dots. This is to see if you can tell the difference between green and red colours, and if you fail, you can't become an airline pilot or an electrician. Not that I want to be either, cos actually I want to be a famous scientist and most of them wear specs anyway.

Think I'll give up telly in case Mum's right and it's too much watching which has strained my eyes…no, forget that.

Thursday 12th December Went with Sam and some friends to see an '18' film – my first try at getting in, so was dead scared, even though my birthday's on Sunday when I'll be 15. We fixed to buy a ticket for John, cos although he's the oldest of us all – 16 next month – his eyes hardly came up to the level of the ticket-selling place, which we thought might cause him problems! All went fine till the wimp checking the tickets on the way in asked John if he was standing in a hole or something, and said if not, then he wasn't going in. Had to flash his ID, so missed our daily quota of visual sex.

John said it made him furious, as a teacher at school had already asked him that day what the weather was like 'down there'. Knew how he felt, as I am sure I'm going to get teased about my specs if I need them. Told him about growth hormone treatment but it turns out he's already had all the tests.

Saturday 14th December Trip to the optician – a shop in the High Street that I had cycled past every day without noticing. One can be blind in more ways than one.

The optician made me sit in a chair in a dark room filled with funny lights and gadgets. Had to tell her which lines in something looking like a cartwheel were clearest, then read from all sorts of different charts while she popped pieces of glass into frames in front of my eyes (like coins going into a slot machine). She smelt nice (unlike many I could name). Then she took a close look into my eyes with a light she called an 'ophthalmoscope', the same as the doctor used in the hospital when I had my accident and at home when I had my headaches. (Had to look up spelling in my dictionary.)

After lots of tests, turned out I am short-sighted and will need glasses or contact lenses – no surprise there. Optician lady helped by saying that each of us is made slightly different from everyone else (and thank goodness for that). But just as some people are short and some are tall, so some are born with eyeballs one shape and some with them another. (Wonder how far these differences go?) She said that it is not that eyes are 'bad' or 'good', but that everyone sees more or less clearly, and if you already see fairly clearly, then you don't need glasses, but the less clearly you see, the more you need them.

Two main reasons for needing glasses are being SHORT-SIGHTED, which is what I am, and means that things far away look blurred, but things close up look clear (like looking at *Practical Photography*!). LONG-SIGHTED is when you can see things far away clearly (like the numbers on the bus, long before it reaches you), but can't see clearly the words in a book or newspaper.

Optician lady said it was OK watching TV, as there is no evidence that this or reading in poor light strains the eyes (said reading in poor light just makes it difficult to read). She also told me that most headaches have nothing to do with bad eyesight.

Then had to choose some frames, as I wanted some that made me look clever but not an actual boff. Seems stupid having a whole lot of boring-looking glasses, as it isn't going to help to encourage people like me to wear them. Lady optician said I needed two pairs, cos I was bound to break or lose one sometime. Bet Mum £5 I wouldn't lose mine. Will put the money towards saving for contact lenses, which Mum says are too expensive for her to get for me at the moment.

Sunday 15th December Cills left my birthday supper with Randy Joe – ooooh…ouch. He's always on the pull. Sam said she was only going out with him because she felt sorry for him – but what about me and my feelings?

Wednesday 18th December What a way to spend the first morning of the holidays. No lie-in till midday and cooking myself an egg or two, with bacon and fried toast, after everybody else has gone out. This morning it was up at nine, for a last glance at my face without pebbles. I'm off to the optician's. Won't wear my glasses on the way home, in case anyone I know sees me. How am I going to break this to Cills?

Thursday 19th December Only wore my new glasses inside the house. Susie said they looked good in such a sarky way it was impossible to believe her. Mum and Dad were encouraging though, especially Dad who now has a 'glasses ally' in the family. Says he can't read the lottery numbers without his glasses – just has to guess, explaining why he's never won anything. Noticed a red mark around the top of my nose where the glasses sit, something else to screw up my appearance. Dad said it often happens like that when you first get specs, but gradually my skin will get used to them.

Saturday 21st December Met Cills Christmas shopping in town. She liked my glasses – and me…for once. Even asked me to a party tonight at her cousin's. Is she just asking me cos she feels sorry for me? Not sure I want to go after what happened at the last party we were at together.

19

Drunken Desires

Wednesday 25th December Tore out last two pages of diary. It's evening on Christmas Day. What I'd written before was too confused (like me), so am starting again, to try and sort things out. All churned up and can't cope. It's to do with Cills, me, and parties, and what to do next, or whether to do anything – all mixed up with me supposed to be feeling good cos it's Christmas. That's what started the whole problem off.

The reason I hadn't wanted to go to the party with Cills was cos the last party I'd been to was pretty boring. This was partly because everybody was drinking and I wasn't, partly cos some gatecrashers came and ruined it, and partly cos everyone else had a girlfriend or boyfriend. But this time Cills was asking me. Mum said that I ought to go as I couldn't be unsociable all my life (wanna bet?).

Was the first time I'd been to a party knowing only one person. Till now, had only been to parties with lots of people the same age as me, like all my friends at school, so on the whole they've been friendly and unthreatening. This one was different. Cills's cousin was 18, so Cills and I were the youngest by far, and personally I felt totally different from everyone else and didn't fit in, especially as Cills knew everybody, and immediately went off leaving me in total isolation.

The party was in this huge room, and I had to walk across it to a table, around which most of these strangers were sitting. At first I felt very self-conscious cos I thought they were all staring at me, but soon realized they were in fact totally ignoring me. Began to panic inside, when to my relief Cills suddenly appeared and offered me a drink. Just took what was offered and drank it down, almost without noticing what it was cos I was so nervous and so anxious to fit in. No one spoke to me, and I couldn't think of anything to say to them. Someone filled my glass from a bottle, and to cover my embarrassment and give me something to do, I kept gulping it down.

Then someone offered me some lime vodka stuff, which I'd never had before, and gulped that down too. The combination of drinks and music made me feel more relaxed, and I started talking to someone who knew some people I knew. Was only as I got up to go and have a pee that I realized how drunk I was. Knew I shouldn't drink any more even if it did relax me and make me able to talk. Suddenly seemed to lose my shyness entirely and began to laugh hysterically at something someone said. Cills came over looking real annoyed and told me to shut up, but I just made things worse by talking a whole lot of furious rubbish to her.

As I talked, I began to collapse and feel incredibly ill. Sat down, with my head between my knees, feeling all cold, sweaty and horrible. Thought I must be dying, I felt so ill…had to lie down. Was convinced Cills would disappear in embarrassment, but actually she was great, and said that she'd ring my dad, and come back with me.

Threw up in the car on the way home. Lucky Cills was sitting in the front. Mum made me drink lots of water, muttering something about 'preventing dehydration', and put me to bed. She was obviously absolutely spare, but didn't say a thing. Don't remember too much after that.

On Christmas Eve stayed in bed till lunchtime. Was totally knackered, and had a splitting headache, and my mouth felt as if someone had shat in it. My first hangover. Could've done without Susie smirking, telling me to 'get a life' and teasing me about getting drunk and about being hot on Cills. Doubted whether Cills even liked me. Fact is I didn't like me after last night. Remembered what a fool I'd made of myself, and knew it was going to ruin Christmas.

Mum and Dad haven't said much about it, though there's an uncomfortable feeling around the house. Wish they'd say SOMETHING. I hung up my stocking, and heard Dad come in at 2 in the morning, stumbling around and leaving a whisky smell behind him.

Today Susie and Sal came in to open their stockings with me. You'd think Sally was past stockings, but I think she wants to believe in Father Christmas even more than we do. Mum cooked a wicked lunch. Noticed Susie had forgotten about being vegetarian. Reckon turkeys don't count.

Subtle Dad gave Susie a drop of wine but not me. Said I'd had enough and didn't fancy having the back of his car stinking of sick again. Think I must've gone red cos Susie gave me one of her smug smiles. It provoked Sally though (who last year had done a special topic on alcohol) into announcing that 9 out of 10 14-year-old children had tasted an alcoholic drink, and that had been at their homes, with their parents' permission. At this, Susie took a 'closely controlled' gulp, spat it out, and said it was disgusting and that she couldn't understand how people drank wine.

Wondered how much of Sal's topic was done from personal experience! Anyhow all this talk of alcohol made me feel sick again, so Sal stopped. Said she'd lend me what she'd written, if I was interested.

Brilliant presents from Mum and Dad – a new Sony, some minidiscs and £20 towards contact lenses. Sal gave me soap, Susie a handkerchief, and the much-needed electric razor came from terrible Uncle Bob. Susie went all sulky cos she didn't get the micro scooter she wanted.

Thursday 26th December Boxing Day. Everyone else seems dead quiet – reckon must be their hangovers. No sympathy from me. Played my new discs. Bored by evening. Read Sally's 'Topic on Alcohol' so I could explain the dangers to my family.

TOPIC ON ALCOHOL by Sally Payne
Form VI Lower

Introduction
Alcohol is a chemical whose formula is C_2H_5OH. It is both a poison and a drug and was around long before Christ was born.

Wonder if Jesus ever got drunk? He seemed to do a bit of turning water into wine when he was short.

It's made by fermentation and can be produced from all kinds of things like potatoes, flowers, berries, etc., but the common alcoholic drinks are wine, which is made from grapes, cider from apples, beer from hops and barley, and gin from barley, malt or rye, flavoured with juniper berries. Rice makes sake, which is Japan's national drink.

A liquid containing just less than 50 per cent of alcohol by weight is called 'proof spirit'. This is because it contains the smallest amount of alcohol which, when gunpowder is

151

soaked in it, would burn. At least one billion gallons of proof spirit are produced each year and mostly used for drinking. A small amount of alcohol will make people more lively, but larger amounts dull their senses and their brains, and they may become unconscious or even die if they take too much.

Reckon that was nearly me.

Pure alcohol is called 'absolute' alcohol and is very difficult to make. The spirit used in industry and for cleaning paintbrushes and things in the home is a mixture of ethyl and methyl alcohol. It is extremely dangerous to drink because the methyl alcohol is so poisonous. Sometimes people have added this to drinks as a joke and other people have been poisoned or blinded, and have even died.

Someone must have done that to my drinks at the Cills party before Christmas.

Facts about Alcoholic Drinks
It's how much pure alcohol there is in a drink that is important, but additives which give drinks their colour, flavour, smell and taste also affect how bad the hangover is. Half a pint of beer or lager = one measure (140 millilitres) of spirits (whisky, gin, vodka, etc.) = a glass of wine = a small glass of sherry = a bit less than half a pint of cider.

Hadn't realized that cider's even stronger than beer. Must be careful how much I drink. Always thought it was weaker, and just tossed it back.

Alcohol is rapidly absorbed from the stomach into the bloodstream; most is burnt up in the liver and the rest is got rid of in sweat and urine. It is more rapidly absorbed on an empty stomach than a full one, and therefore it's better to eat before you drink. In general it takes the body one hour to get rid of one standard drink. More than five drinks at a party and you won't feel all right again till next morning. Drinking two and a half pints of beer or cider, or the equivalent, in an hour puts you over the legal limit for driving.

The Dangers

In the short term, the main danger is that alcohol affects your judgement, self-control and skills. Road accidents after drinking are the commonest cause of death in young men, and one in three drivers killed in road accidents have blood alcohols over the legal limit. The number of innocent people killed or seriously injured each year by drivers with blood alcohol over the legal limit is 3,000. Even AT the legal limit, you are four times more likely to crash.

Hope Sal's shown this to her boyfriend Steve, seeing the way he rides his motorbike.

The long-term effects of alcohol are, among other things: damage to the liver due to inflammation and scarring, bleeding and ulcers in the stomach, cancer of the mouth and throat, brain damage, interference with your sex life, depression, psychiatric disorders, violence.

Just wish Cills would interfere with my sex life.

Drinking in pregnancy can also cause damage to the unborn child, and it may be born very small, wizened, and brain-damaged.

Women's bodies are more affected by alcohol than men's and therefore it does more damage to them.

I wonder if this is because men have more water in their bodies and therefore alcohol would be more diluted than in a woman's body?

> *Drinking in children – some of the facts that I could find:*
> *– 9 out of 10 children try alcohol by the age of 14, and this is the same for boys and girls*
> *– most of these try it at home*
> *– children who smoke also drink more alcohol*
> *– boys tend to drink beer and lager while girls prefer wine and cocktails*
> *– children who are keen on drinking alcohol are more influenced by their friends than by their parents*
> *– boys and girls who drink a lot are seen by their friends as liking clubbing, going out a lot with friends, acting big and showing off, getting into trouble and fighting*
> *– boys and girls who never drink are seen as the opposite*
> *– children who drink a lot are seen as being more disliked by grown-ups than by other children, and those that don't drink at all are the opposite...*

Can see why she got an 'A' for this. Went on for pages and pages, but I'd had enough.

Saturday 28th December Today was OK – snowed a bit. Do really like Cills. Especially after she was so nice when I was drunk. Things are going well for now – messaged me saying 'Hope u r better – luv Cills'. Will she turn up at Sam's New Year's Eve party? Randy Joe's away!

Monday 30th December Holidays are great cos of being able to sleep in. Sam's mum rang to talk to my mum about the party. She thinks everyone will come with bottles of booze, and Sam's dad says he's going to frisk them as they come in. Poor Sam. Dad and Mum asked us at dinner what we thought about drinking alcohol, but ended up as usual by telling us what THEY thought.

Said I didn't think it was right to go down to the pub every night like Nick's dad, who's got this huge beer belly hanging out. Also wouldn't want to turn out like the tramps who hung out down the shopping centre, clutching bottles of cider. Though reckoned it was OK to have the odd drink now and then.

Sal had had her first drink when she was 10. Mum had given her a little white wine and she had pinched the bottle and finished it in her bedroom – though Sal says there wasn't much left. After gulping down what there was, she had felt giddy and as if her head was going to fall off, so she had had to lie down. She had taken it because she had always felt a goody-goody and now wanted to do something against the grain. Really shocked Mum, who had had no idea, but both Mum and Dad had to admit that they got a 'bit merry' sometimes. (Didn't tell them that I'd seen Father Christmas more than a bit 'merry'.)

Sal, when she'd been out of work after failing her exams, had got really depressed and had gone down to the pub all the time, even though she didn't have much money. Now that she was working at the local hairdresser's and had decided to retake some of her exams, she wasn't drinking nearly as much.

Wednesday 1st January NEW YEAR'S DAY – FEEL TERRIFIC! Went to Sam's party with Nick. Turned out we were both dreading it. Nick told me that there are three kinds of parties. 'Snogging ones', where the same music goes on and on as everyone is so into one another that no one wants to get up to change it. 'Booze-ups', where everyone drinks lager or beer, it's mates only, and they all end up smashed and out on the streets, looking for fags or worse and throwing up. The third kind was the worst – 'the school do', with teachers making fools of themselves trying to dance and wearing 'trendy' clothes. No touching drink or each other at these ones!

Nick was only going to have one drink at this one. He'd got smashed at the last party so as not to feel left out, and had found his mouth telling people exactly what he thought of them. Had done the worst thing possible – drunk cider, then wine, then vodka, then beer. Even I could have told him to at least stick to drinking ONE kind of alcohol. He'd ended up lying down in the road with his mate, to see who died first.

Sam's party was great. Terrific music, lots of food and, like Nick, I stuck to one type of drink. Saw the New Year in HEAVY SNOGGING WITH CILLS. After midnight things with Cills got even BETTER. Hope this is a catching disease.

IT MAKES ME FEEL REALLY REALLY GOOD!!!

Index